D0622751

The ESSENCE *of* SANTA FE

From a Way of Life to a Style

Jerilou Hammett

Kingsley Hammett

Peter Scholz

The ESSENCE *of* SANTA FE

From a Way of Life to a Style

Ancient City Press

Santa Fe

Previous Spread: ***The End of the Trail***
by Gerald Cassidy. (MNM #6977)
Right: **Looking east on San Francisco Street
from the Santa Fe Plaza. (MNM #91416)**

First Edition
09 08 07 06 05   5 4 3 2 1

Text ©2006 Kingsley Hammett, Jerilou Hammett
Photographs ©2006 credits noted

All rights reserved. No part of this book may be reproduced by any means whatsoever without written
permission from the publisher, except brief portions quoted for purpose of review.

Published by Ancient City Press
An imprint of Gibbs Smith, Publisher
P.O. Box 667, Layton, Utah 84041
Orders: 1.800.748.5439
www.gibbs-smith.com

Cover Photo: Santa Fe Plaza ca. 1912. Photo by Jesse L. Nusbaum. (MNM #139151)
Back Cover Photos: Top Left: Photo by Bonita Barlow, Middle Left: Photo by Kingsley Hammett
Bottom Left: Photo by Bonita Barlow, Right: Adobe Plastering. Photo by Mildred T. Crews. (MNM #66644)

Designed and produced by Peter Scholz
Printed and bound in Hong Kong

Library of Congress Cataloging-in-Publication Data
Library of Congress Control Number: 2004117909
ISBN 1-58685-406-2

Corpus Christi Procession going down San Francisco Street in 1895. (MNM #15252)

This book is dedicated to the many
Santa Feans who continue to maintain
their essential way of life, their values,
their humility, their dignity, their
traditions, and their sense of humor
in the face of the challenges posed by
unbridled growth and its accompanying
materialism. It is the spirit — the warmth,
the hospitality, and the beauty — of this
culture that is the essence of Santa Fe.

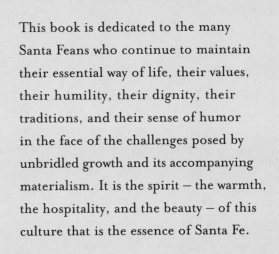

CONTENTS

Left: **Bird's-eye view of Santa Fe,
1882. (MNM #23306)**

The Santa Fe Plaza has been the center of community life for almost four hundred years. (MNM #11299)

The concept of Santa Fe "style" was a fabrication from its inception. It was invented nearly a century ago specifically to attract tourists. Today's incarnation bears little connection to its predecessor and has virtually no historic value. It is simply another attempt to sell Santa Fe. And sell it does: lots of books, lots of painted coyotes, lots of *piñon* incense burners, hotel rooms, and faux adobe houses. Underneath the marketing, however, Santa Fe is still just an unpretentious town where most people live a simple life, eking out a modest living, raising families, observing the same traditions they always have while paying no attention to the swirl of real estate and tourist hype that rages around them. There is no dress code. There is no social register. And almost everything that passes for architectural purity is a compromise.

Santa Fe is a way of life, not a style. It is a set of deeply held traditions and values, not a marketable item. It is a people steeped in strong family relationships and abiding religious faith. It is an aesthetic rooted in the natural rhythms of daily life; it speaks of a simple order, in concert with nature, shaped by the climate, and framed by the seasons. Here, local people still clean the *acequia*, gather wood in the mountains, collect *piñon* nuts, roast *chiles*, roll *tortillas*, and always have time for family, for time in their scale of values is more valuable than money.

The essence of Santa Fe can be grasped only through an understanding of the qualities that inform it. It speaks to you on a cold winter's night when the soft glow of a kitchen light, a glint of the moon on fresh-fallen snow, and the tang of burning *piñon* warm your heart

and spirit. It is visible in the soft turn of an adobe wall and the sight of two friends stopping in the middle of the road to visit through their car windows while patient drivers wait quietly behind.

The true Santa Fe is revealed through its imperfection: like the New Mexico landscape, it is coarse and flawed up close but faultless from a distance. There are no right angles. There are no unblemished surfaces. There is no uniformity. There is just an organic sense of how elements come together and play their individual roles in a greater harmony. This is Santa Fe.

The essence of Santa Fe grew out of history, out of the lessons learned from the neighboring Pueblo Indians who taught the Spanish settlers how to adapt to isolation and necessity. The lessons were about simplicity, humility, functionality, and especially ingenuity. People here had to use what they found — earth, stones, wood, straw, water, bones — to make the things they needed. Everything they created had a function; nothing was gratuitous. Homes were small and clustered together into compounds for mutual support and safety and to keep the family close. They grew organically to serve specific needs. Streets followed goat paths and water courses. Out of this has grown a charming city with an Old World feeling.

We have written this book to challenge the misconceptions fostered by the marketing of this thing called Santa Fe "style." There is an undeniable magic to this old city that still can be found if one looks hard enough. We hope this book serves as a guide to that magic and the essence of Santa Fe.

CHAPTER 1

FROM THE PUEBLO PERSPECTIVE

A FUNDAMENTAL UNDERSTANDING OF CONNECTEDNESS AND ONENESS WITH THE LAND, THE PLACE, AND ALL OTHER BEINGS ALLOWED EARLY PUEBLO PEOPLE TO SURVIVE IN THE SOUTHWEST FOR THOUSANDS OF YEARS BEFORE EUROPEANS ARRIVED HERE. PUEBLO PEOPLE KNEW THAT A DEEP APPRECIATION AND ACKNOWLEDGMENT OF PLACE AS AN INTERDEPENDENT WHOLE WAS NECESSARY TO LIVE IN THIS BEAUTIFUL BUT HARSH ENVIRONMENT. THEY HONORED THE SKY AND CLOUDS FOR LIFE-GIVING RAIN. THEY THANKED THE MOUNTAINS FOR THEIR WORLD-DEFINING POSTURES. THE LAND ITSELF WAS LIFE. IT WAS THE MOTHER THROUGH WHICH ALL LIFE FLOWED.

These acknowledgments were the basis of traditional Pueblo village organization and house form. The built environment was a reflection of the order found in nature, and it was designed to continuously remind people of their essential relationship to the earth, the sky, the wind, and the water. Architectural details and elements were significant only as symbols of a larger connection to the natural environment.

All life, as well as the built environment, swirled around the center, the *nansipu*, or "middle-heart place." This center was the opening into other levels of existence within the womb of the earth. Pueblo people believed that they emerged through this earth womb to dwell at the level between the earth and the sky, between male and female.

Surrounding this female center point was the plaza, or *bupingeh*, an open yet contained communal space, also identified as female. Around that were arranged the houses, whose two- and three-story terraced forms reflected the containing, protective quality of the distant hills and mountains associated with maleness.

From the female opening of the mother in the plaza to the interconnected houses surrounding it, to the animal corrals, to the trash mounds and the fields beyond, to the male hills and far mountains, the community flowed in concentric rings to the outer limits of the Pueblo world.

Within the plaza each pueblo had a community house, or *kiva*. While the *kiva* has become in recent decades more reserved for religious ceremonies, it was historically a place (especially in times of bad weather) for the everyday chores of cleaning the harvest, weaving blankets, preparing and consuming food, and socializing. These same tasks, including drying fruits and vegetables, grinding and cooking corn, and baking bread, took place in the open plaza when the skies were fair. Other activities, including sleeping, playing, and just watching each other, took place on rooftops. All outdoor space within the pueblo was considered community space, and residents moved freely across rooftops and within the plaza.

The houses were built of stone set in mud mortar, or mud mixed with either ashes or dried plant material, all of which were symbolic to the Pueblo people. In the Tewa language, the word *nung* meant both "us" and "earth," implying that the people were both born and made of the same material as their houses. Everyone engaged in house building — men, women, children, and the elderly. Dwellings flowed seamlessly out of the surrounding earth, often with nothing to distinguish the walls from the ground out of which they grew. Children mixed clay, water, and straw in a pit with their feet, women built and plastered the walls with mud, and men harvested and

put in place the heavy log roof supports. All things related to the home — including house maintenance — were the province of the women and children.

The rooms were dark, with few if any windows, the better to store food. They were small to facilitate winter heating. They served many functions, with little regard for the European concept of separation of space for work, meals, sleep, and the need for privacy. Privacy was something everyone carried around within himself, and there was no need for walls to defend it.

Sharing was paramount. The kitchen was used for cooking, eating, and receiving guests. As members of a subsistence farming society, Pueblo people placed great importance on storerooms that doubled as sleeping and living areas. An abiding trust in the natural world extended to other human beings, and consequently there was no need to guard one's possessions against theft.

Pueblo people had a very different relationship with their houses than did Europeans. Houses in no way symbolized power and wealth but were simple and functional expressions of the human need for shelter. Architectural details such as doors, windows, and trim held little importance for their decorative value, and the individual house unit was not as important as the community form and the concept of its wholeness.

Santa Clara Pueblo.
(MNM #42780)

In the Native world everything had its cycle, including a building, and its occupants were intimately involved with its creation, its life, and its inevitable death. A house was built to meet a specific need and was allowed to disintegrate back into the earth when that need no longer existed. Until then it was a live, organic, animate being, and its death was just part of the anticipated cycle. When you walked into a Pueblo house you could sense its personality, feel its breath, and taste its essence. Houses, like people, were periodically fed, healed, and blessed. Offerings usually were placed in the four corners at the start of construction, and as a house took shape, more prayers were said and offerings placed within the walls and ceiling. Ancestors were often buried in the floor, and their spirits lived on in the house. With every living breath the current occupants took in the energies surrounding them, with every exhalation they put out some of themselves, and the house followed a similar pattern. If cracks developed in the walls, the house signaled its time to return to the earth and was allowed a dignified death. Its bricks crumbled into a pile, and their mud ultimately melted back into the earth. Such materials as could be salvaged were then recycled into a new house.

After the Spanish arrived in 1598, the Pueblo lifestyle, social unit, and building form began to change. The colonizers brought with them the notion of personal ownership of land and material goods, an idea unknown to earlier Pueblo people. Over time the sense of community oneness was replaced first by the extended family and then by the nuclear family. The Spanish also limited the Pueblo world to a radius of six miles from the front of the mission church they had forced upon the Pueblo people. The Native Americans' sense of fluidity and their relationship to the concentric wholeness of their environment were ultimately lost and replaced by the static quality of ownership in this newly confined world. People began to see themselves as owning their fields, owning their houses, owning a portion of the community. The extended family replaced the community unit, and certain sections of the plaza became identified with certain families. Eventually, people stayed off the rooftops and away from the front of houses identified with other families, and the plaza ceased to be a communal place.

Modern Santa Fe is built over the ruins of prehistoric Pueblo villages. Yet the old Pueblo idea that the *po-wa-ha*, or breath of the cosmos that connects all living beings, including houses, remains. It may not permeate the structure of the modern city, but the land retains the memory of a people deeply respectful of the surrounding mountains, the billowing clouds, and the winds that keep life in flux.

Left: **Santa Clara Pueblo.**
(Detail of MNM #42780)
Below: **Acoma Pueblo.**
(MNM #2052)

STEP DESIGN

Pueblo people believed that they emerged from the center of the earth, the womb, through a hole in the middle of the plaza to dwell at the level between the earth and the sky. Consequently, one of the more recognizable features of early Pueblo home and village construction was the step that symbolized the many levels of existence within their spirit world. At the same time steps and ladders served as practical elements. Residents climbed up to reach the top of the *kiva* before descending into its interior. They climbed a ladder or adobe steps built into a wall to reach the roof of the next level of housing before descending another ladder into the rooms below. By first climbing and then descending steps and ladders, Pueblo Indians continually reenacted the return to their place of origin.

Pueblo houses were usually built in a two- and three-story terraced style that formed a series of giant steps to reflect the embracing and protective quality of the distant hills and mountains associated with maleness. Mountains contained the valley, the houses contained the plaza, and the plaza contained the people. All of this served to symbolize the connection between the physical world and the spirit world; the world of the Pueblo people and the world of nature; the continuous movement from one level of existence to another; the constant flux and change of life; and the concept of safety, protection, and containment. Today this same step feature can be seen on any number of Santa Fe houses, parapets, and garden walls, although this modern iteration of an ancient belief system has no connection to its original significance.

Above: **Steps and ladders on Pueblo houses symbolized the connection between the physical world and the spirit world. Acoma Pueblo. (MNM #2051)**
Right: **Acoma Pueblo. (McNutt Collection, NM State Records and Archives #5753)**

THE PUEBLO FORM

Central to Pueblo belief was the constant reference to and replication of the natural world in everything they built. Their goal was to be in touch with nature and natural forms at all times and to try to make things as beautiful as nature does. This is reflected in both the path up to Acoma (opposite page) that was cut into the hillside between towering walls of rock and a passageway formed between houses at Laguna Pueblo (left). At Zuni Pueblo, similar passageways were covered, which further helped channel the breezes and reminded pueblo members that the buildings were organic, breathing, living and dying entities.

Opposite Page: **Trail, Acoma Pueblo.
(Detail of MNM #144519)**
This Page: **Laguna Pueblo.
(Detail of MNM #144715)**

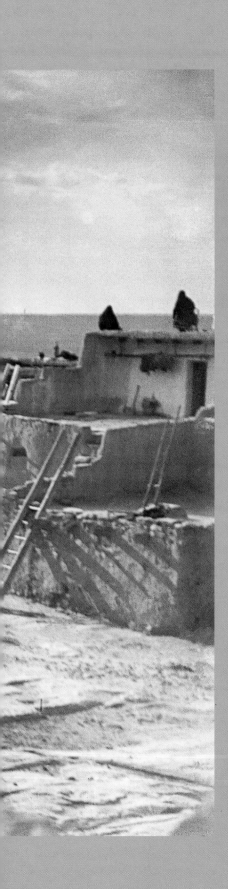

INSIDE THE PUEBLO

Pueblo homes were built as stacked forms, set back to mirror the shape of surrounding mountains. At Taos Pueblo, near the base of the highest mountain in the state, the houses soar to four and five stories, while in riverside pueblos like Santa Clara, the buildings never went above two stories, mimicking the lower profile of the nearby hills. Regardless of the building height, the way the houses enclosed a plaza remained constant. And the interplay between a series of dualities – male and female, container and contained, summer and winter, north and south – all played out within the plaza form.

Left: **Stacked houses reflected the surrounding hills and mountains. Acoma Pueblo. (MNM #144511)**
Above: **At Taos Pueblo the houses soared to four and five stories. (MNM #16096)**

BUILDING AND PLASTERING

The Pueblo world was very gender specific, and it was acknowledged that each person had his or her place. The men (and boys over the age of twelve) were in the fields or out hunting in the mountains, while women and children were in the village. Yet there was significant crossover and mutual support. At the time of a particularly bountiful harvest, the women would bring food to the men in the fields and lend their hand to gathering in the crop. Likewise, men helped build houses by bringing the heavy roof beams from the mountains and mixing mud for walls. But it was the women and children who assumed responsibility for maintaining the home and applying its annual coat of protective mud plaster.

Opposite Page: **Pueblo women were responsible for the maintenance of their adobe homes.** (MNM #41589)
This Page: **Plastering, San Ildefonso Pueblo.** (MNM #43611)

PRODUCING AND PROCESSING FOOD

In the arid high desert, Pueblo Indians either dry-farmed their lands or diverted irrigation water from the rivers. At Zuni Pueblo they developed waffle gardens (like the French Intensive method of raised beds), where they cultivated their crops in small squares enclosed by wood and adobe forms to retain precious water. Harvesting and food preparation were communal affairs often conducted in the center of the plaza, in the *kiva*, and on the rooftops. *Ramadas* — shade structures made of poles covered with brush — were built in the fields and within the pueblo plaza to both provide vital shade and serve as places to hang, dry, and store corn, *chile*, and herbs.

Above: **Crops at Zuni Pueblo were grown in waffle gardens.** (MNM #8742)

Opposite Page: **Vast quantities of food were stored in the plaza at Santa Clara Pueblo.** (Detail of MNM #42784

Above: **Shucking corn was a communal effort at San Juan Pueblo. (Detail of MNM #3984)**

CORN AND WHEAT

Primary to the Pueblo diet were beans and squash, wild game and birds. But nothing held more significance than corn, and a bountiful crop made them feel all was right with the world. Corn symbolized the life source itself. The figure that represents the power of corn is always shown with an erect penis and a bag of seeds slung over his shoulder in an explicit sexual reference to pro-creation and the continuation of life. Corn was air dried, roasted fresh, and baked into *chicos*. It was ground into meal and made into a mush that had the consistency of rice. The mush was poured over a hot stone, cooked like a thin *tortilla*, and rolled into *piki*, a breadlike hand food. More finely ground corn meal was diluted in water for a drink called *atole*. After the arrival of the Spanish, the Pueblos embraced the new foods brought north from Mexico, including fruits, *chile*, and wheat. They learned to thresh grain under the hooves of circling livestock, winnow it in the wind, and wash it in the river in large baskets.

Top Right: **Wheat cleaners, San Juan Pueblo. (Detail of MNM #144548)** Bottom Right: **Washing wheat, Jémez Pueblo. (Detail of MNM #42075)**

This Page: **Jewelry making, Zuni Pueblo. (Detail of MNM #9189)**
Opposite Page: **Potter María Martinez, San Ildefonso Pueblo. (MNM #73453)**

NATIVE AMERICAN ARTS

Until the railroads penetrated the Southwest in the 1880s, Indian arts, including pottery, basketry, and weaving, were associated with the utilitarian and ceremonial needs of daily living. And no matter what they made, they did so with their own aesthetic sensibilities in the best way they knew how, always incorporating design elements that replicated the natural world around them. But once the railroad brought with it commercial replacements for Native-made objects along with curious tourists fascinated by Native Americans and hungry for Indian-made souvenirs, their work became more decorative and suited to what the tourists wanted to buy. Dwindling rainfall and shrinking crops forced the Native population into the white man's cash economy and left them all too willing to re-create their arts for the small income that provided. By the 1920s both Indian and Anglo artists were making money depicting a long-lost way of life, and the formation of what would become the Southwestern Association for Indian Arts launched the annual Santa Fe Indian Market. Today it is the nation's largest Native arts fair. Functional and ceremonial art has now virtually disappeared from the Pueblo communities, replaced by items that are valued simply for their beauty and economic value.

JEWELRY

Ancient sites near the village of Cerrillos (south of Santa Fe) are considered the most extensive prehistoric turquoise mining operations in North America. Pueblo Indians were fascinated by the idea that the bluish stones captured the mystery of the sky above them. Centuries before the Navajos adopted the art of silverwork, which had been brought north from Mexico by the Spanish, the Zunis were working turquoise, jet, coral, and shell (which came to play a prominent role in Pueblo myths) into long strands of thinly sliced disks called *heishi*. After the introduction of silver, the Pueblos bent the gleaming metal to their own meaning and symbolism, and hammered thin pieces into the delicate petals of the squash blossom. Over time certain pieces and styles became identified with specific pueblos and reflected their sense of location, proportion, tradition, and relationship.

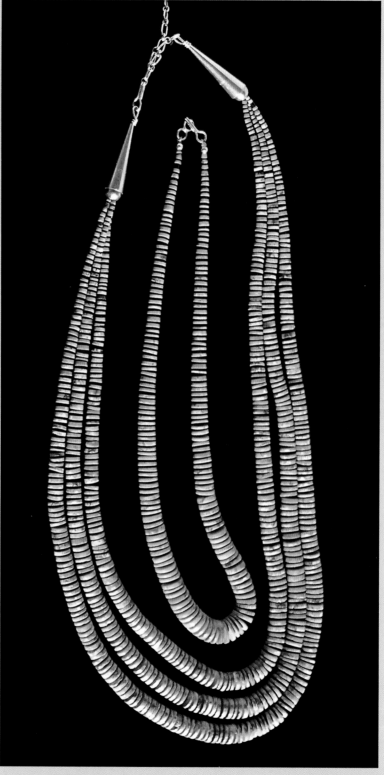

Opposite Page Left: **Woman, Isleta Pueblo. (Detail of MNM #144705)** This Page Left: **Person, Zuni Pueblo. (Detail of MNM #144735)** Above: **Squash blossom necklace, Zuni Pueblo. (MNM #756)**

BASKETS

The art of basketry was such an important part of Pueblo life that early archaeologists and anthropologists, who found examples dating back 10,000 years, referred to their creators as the Basket Makers. At one time all Pueblo Indians made their own baskets, which fulfilled a variety of functions, from collecting berries to washing wheat to transporting grain to sifting flour. In more recent times the practice has been abandoned by most Pueblo peoples, with the exception of the Hopi and Jémez, and is being revived at places like the Poeh Arts Center in Pojoaque Pueblo.

Left: **Hopi basket maker.**
(MNM #37530)

WEAVING

Long before the Spanish brought sheep and wool to New Mexico, Pueblo Indians were cultivating cotton and weaving cloth for garments, sashes, hair ties, and blankets. Like their pottery, the woven sashes incorporated designs drawn from nature, such as the steps of multilevel mountains and the tassels that symbolized rain, all of which were contained within a thin border of black thread.

Below: **Weaver, Cochití Pueblo. (Detail of MNM #2286)**

POTTERY

Pottery, the most ubiquitous of Native American arts, can be found in every pueblo. While traditional pottery throughout the Southwest begins with a simple coil of clay, the work of different pueblos can be readily identified by particular styles and distinctive designs, dictated in part by the locally available clay, local tradition and sensibility, and the symbolism of each particular pueblo. One shared characteristic is the attempt to replicate nature – the complementary geometric juxtaposition between black and white, male and female, leaves, flowers, lightning bolts, birds' eyes, and animals taking in the breath of life. Patterns that encircle a pot signify one context held within another context and the unbroken continuity of the life cycle. Each vessel is bound and contained by a thin line around the rim, much like the black border of the woven sash or the houses that enclose the plaza.

Left: **Taos Pueblo, woman carrying Santa Clara pot. (Detail of MNM #144536)**

CHAPTER 2

THE SPANISH CONQUEST

A S THE *CONQUISTADORES* MARCHED NORTH UP THE RÍO GRANDE VALLEY IN 1598 AT THE HEAD OF A COLUMN OF SOME 600 SETTLERS AND THOUSANDS OF LIVESTOCK, THEY MUST HAVE MADE A FEARSOME SIGHT. HEAVILY ARMED WITH STEEL DAGGERS, SWORDS, AND HARQUEBUSES, AND HEAVILY ARMORED FROM THEIR HELMETS TO THEIR STEEL-CAPPED STIRRUPS, THESE STRANGERS WERE ABOUT TO ALTER FOREVER THE PEACEFUL, STABLE LIFE THAT PUEBLO INDIANS HAD ENJOYED FOR CENTURIES. IT IS NO WONDER THAT IN THE TEWA LANGUAGE THE WORD FOR SPANISH IS THE SAME AS THAT FOR "METAL."

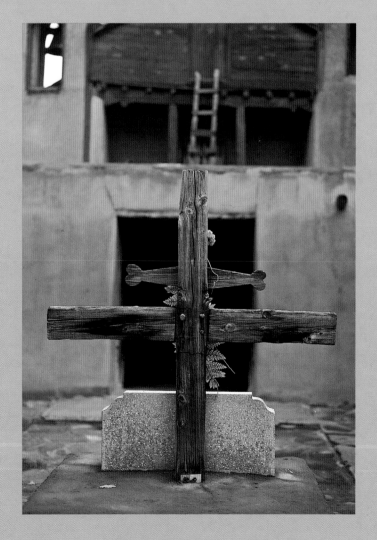

After an initial settlement under the leadership of Don Juan de Oñate failed near San Juan Pueblo, the Spanish founded the permanent capital of the northernmost province of New Spain in 1610 in what is present-day Santa Fe. The community was laid out in accordance with the Laws of the Indies, a set of town planning principles issued by King Philip II in 1573. These laws accompanied all expeditions to the New World and dictated the location, layout, form, and settlement pattern of all colonial cities. The resulting Villa Real de Santa Fe de San Francisco de Asís may lack the colonial grandeur of Latin American capitals, but it followed the same urban plan. Generations of visitors to Santa Fe have been struck by her beautiful setting high on a desert plateau at the base of a majestic mountain range, with its crisp air, brilliant sunlight, and endless vistas across a broad river valley into stunning sunsets. They are charmed by the calm,

Above: *Conquistador* Francisco Vásquez de Coronado, painting by Gerald Cassidy. (MNM #20206)

generous, tree-shaded Plaza, the magnificent cathedral at one end overlooking the town from its slight elevation, the stolid government building running along the Plaza's northern edge, and the commercial downtown with sidewalks sheltered by *portales*. None of it occurred by accident.

As instructed by royal decree, founding Governor Don Pedro de Peralta sited the new community in a fertile, well-watered area some distance from the Native populations he was sent to Christianize. At its center he placed a rectangular plaza, which was supposed to be one-and-a-half times as long as it was wide to accommodate fiestas and horse-mounted military drills. Giving the site of the church the highest priority, Peralta located it at the eastern edge of the Plaza, set upon elevated ground reached by steps so that it would stand above surrounding buildings and be visible from all angles. He built the *casas reales*, or government buildings, along the northern perimeter of the Plaza, making sure they did not interfere with or block the view of the church. The buildings originally ringing the plaza were occupied by wealthy families in the absence of the commercial activity that would follow. These buildings were fronted with *portales* to give residents a sheltered place to congregate and trade.

A grid of residential streets stretched

outward from the Plaza. Beyond them lay irrigated fields and orchards that backed up to the stunning 12,000-plus-foot Sangre de Cristo mountains, which stood as a natural protective barrier and whose flanks turned red under the setting sun.

Much has changed in downtown Santa Fe in 400 years, but most of the original pattern is still visible. The Plaza has become considerably smaller than originally established, but the cathedral still commands the high ground, and the Palace of the Governors remains where first built. The downtown street grid still exists (although close-in residential areas have been given over to commercial

uses), while the farmlands and orchards have been filled in with houses, and the once free-running Santa Fe River has been dammed into a reservoir.

When Governor Peralta built the Palace of the Governors, it was a sprawling adobe-brick structure of many rooms with towers at its corners. He used conscripted Native labor despite the prohibitions against it in the Laws of the Indies. The government fortress — which originally ran from what is now Palace Avenue north to Federal Place — served as a corral for Peralta's horses, quartered his soldiers (and their families), and housed government offices.

CHURCH DOMINATION

Religion dominated life in colonial Santa Fe. In 1622, on the high ground at the eastern edge of the Plaza, rose a church and monastery, built of adobe bricks. It was destroyed in the Pueblo Revolt of 1680 and was rebuilt by 1714. Known thereafter as La Parroquia, or "the parish church" (left), it had crenellated walls and twin towers that echoed those of a Moorish castle. Beginning in 1869 the formal Romanesque Revival Saint Francis Cathedral was built around and over La Parroquia. When the Cathedral was completed in 1884, the walls of La Parroquia were dismantled and the adobe bricks carried out through the front door. Today Saint Francis Cathedral remains the city's most dignified building.

During the initial settlement period, another church was built on the south side of the Santa Fe River. Known as San Miguel (below), it was for the use of the Christianized Mexican-Indian servants who accompanied the early Spanish settlers but lived separately from them in Barrio Analco. It too was partially destroyed in the Pueblo Revolt and rebuilt on the same site with a three-tiered bell tower and adobe battlements. Although it has been remodeled several times since, it retains many authentic details – richly carved beams, corbels, and choir loft railings. These features would find their way into Santa Fe homes during the period of architectural revival in the early twentieth century.

Left: **Santa Fe Plaza and La Parroquia. (Detail of MNM #103021)** Below: **San Miguel Church. (MNM #15856)**

MISSIONARIES

Above: **Mission church at Acoma Pueblo. (MNM #148154)** Opposite Page Right: **San Geronimo de Taos Church.** Opposite Page Left: **Mission church at Santa Clara Pueblo. (MNM #31520)**

The history of early New Mexico can best be described as an ongoing conflict between missionaries and rebels. Franciscan friars who accompanied Peralta came to claim souls for the church. They soon fanned out across the landscape and, pueblo by pueblo, conscripted native labor to build Catholic missions. Early examples at Pecos and Acoma followed a form first developed in Mexico during the 1500s. Each church was massive, long, and narrow, built in the shape of a cross, and made of a mixture of adobe bricks and stone set in mud mortar. Unlike the Pueblo *kiva* that represented the connection with the center of the earth, the Spanish mission churches had towers that reached up to the heavens to project the glory of God and the power of the Catholic Church. Giant peeled-log *vigas* held up the roof. Elaborately carved corbels supported the beams where they met the wall.

Metal woodworking tools brought by the Spanish — saws, axes, chisels, augers, and adzes — made this ornamental detailing possible. This highly evolved form of craftsmanship was unknown to the Pueblo people and never took hold in the simple homes of the Spanish settlers. The Franciscan friars introduced the idea of carving wood for its own sake, which gave the buildings a sense of man-made beauty unknown to Natives to whom a roof beam

held up the cosmos. The missions were dimly lit by natural light from tiny windows glazed with selenite and mica and simple wooden cross-bar candle holders called *arenas*, which were raised and lowered by ropes from the *vigas* overhead. Attached to one side of the church would be the *convento*, a row of single rooms that enclosed a courtyard with an orchard and garden. Here the friars lived and conducted religious as well as vocational training for the Indians.

Above: **Massive posts, corbels, and beams allowed for the large expanses of mission churches. Zuni Pueblo. (Detail of MNM #61752)**

POSTS AND BEAMS

Many of the elaborate design elements introduced by the Spanish and perfected by the friars who built the Catholic missions and churches throughout the Río Grande Valley eventually found their way into wealthy residences. These included carved posts and beams and corbels cut in a variety of geometric profiles. In a land where everything was made from the same mud blocks, the durable posts, beams, and corbels served two functions: they allowed for larger spans, and thus larger spaces, and they provided a place to add decoration and individual expression.

Ceilings too became expressive elements. The spaces between the beams were filled with different materials and patterns. Two of the most common were rows of peeled aspen poles laid in a herringbone pattern and lengths of rough split cedar.

Centuries later, when Santa Fe leaders sought to revive the traditional local architecture, they combed the churches for examples of the most sophisticated forms of this vernacular style. These features appear today all over the city.

Above: **Contemporary buildings mimic the architectural elements of old Spanish mission churches.**

Above: **Elaborately carved posts and corbels at the convent at San Ildefonso mission church. (Detail of MNM #12399)**

Below: **A matched pair of posts, beams, and corbels at Taos Church. (Detail of MNM #59293)**

CARVED CORBELS

Corbels displayed a wide variety of designs and artistic expressions. Beyond their function of supporting heavy beams, they lent great creative articulation to an otherwise plain building form. With saws and chisels, early New Mexican craftsmen cut their corbel ends into profiles and decorated their surfaces with geometric and flowered designs and bullet carving.

Opposite Page Right: **Corbels and beams in mission churches such as these at Santa Cruz were massive. (MNM #13921)** This Page Left: **Carved corbel, Zuni Pueblo. (MNM #61745)**

DECORATIVE CARVING

Chip carving was the simplest form of ornamentation that could turn a plain wooden beam into a work of art. It was often combined with other geometric and floral motifs to create elaborate statements.

Opposite Page Top: **Geometric carvings decorate the beams at San Ildefonso Pueblo. (MNM #13919)**
Opposite Page Bottom: **Painted chip carving on corbel and beam.**
This Page: **Rosettes and bullets carved into beams at San Miguel Church.**

CHOIR LOFTS
AND RAILINGS

Another architectural element of the mission churches was the choir loft. It usually spanned the rear of the building over the main entrance and was reached by a ladder. The loft was made of a row of beams held up by posts and carved corbels and was enclosed by a railing with carved spindles. Today these details are found in private homes as both mezzanines and balconies. The carved spindles are also found on stair railings, window and door grilles, and radiator covers.

Above: **Choir loft above the entrance of the Acoma Pueblo Mission. (MNM #37843)**
Right: **The church choir loft became a design element that was incorporated into the homes of the wealthy.**

Above: **The balcony at the Amelia White residence looks very much like the choir lofts of the mission churches. (Detail of MNM #69633)**

PUEBLO REVOLT

After seventy years of forced labor, forced religion, forced tribute, floggings, famine, disease, and general abuse, the Native Americans rose up in revolt in 1680 under the leadership of a San Juan Pueblo Indian medicine man named Popé. The story goes that he sent word south from Taos to Isleta that the date for the general uprising would be August 10. But on August 8, Spanish Governor Don Antonio Otermín arrested two of the messengers and forced them to reveal the plot. This propelled the Pueblo Indians to put their plan into effect the following morning, beginning at Tesuque and spreading throughout the day to more far-flung pueblos. At least 1,000 Spaniards living in and around Santa Fe gathered for safety in the patio of the Palace of the Governors, and the rooftop was ringed with armed soldiers. Here they spent the next five days waiting for the expected attack. It came after Governor Otermín rejected the Indians' demand that all settlers and friars leave the province immediately. The Indians burned the San Miguel Church and engaged a troop of Spanish soldiers in a pitched battle on the southern outskirts of town. As the Indians retreated in near defeat, Native reinforcements arrived from the north. They burned the church on the Plaza and cut off the water supply to the Spaniards hiding within the walls of the presidio. On the morning of August 20, the Spaniards rushed from the royal houses and put 1,500 Indians to flight. But from Indian captives Governor Otermín learned that in the previous ten days the rest of his province had been devastated.

Concluding that his band of survivors in Santa Fe was in a perilous situation, he decided to abandon the burned-out town. He gathered up the settlement's religious articles, distributed the remaining clothing and supplies to his charges, and began marching south the next day toward Isleta and on to El Paso before the Indians could regroup. The Indians immediately retook what was left of Santa Fe and obeyed the orders of Popé to throw away their rosaries and crosses; to never speak the names of Jesus, Mary, or the saints; to renounce their Christian wedding vows and take up with new partners if they chose; to stop speaking Spanish; and to burn all the churches and Catholic symbols. The Indians killed some twenty-one Franciscan friars and approximately 400 of the 2,500 colonists in the fighting. They enclosed the Plaza with three- and four-story houses that sheltered about 1,500 people, and built two large *kivas* in its center. There they remained for the next twelve years, until Don Diego de Vargas led a group of Spaniards up the Camino Real in 1692 to once again occupy the land for the Spanish crown.

The Pueblo Indian Revolt was the only successful revolution by indigenous people in North America. Today a bust of Popé sits in honor in the rotunda of the nation's Capitol, and the legacy of the revolution may be seen in the relatively peaceful coexistence that has prevailed between the pueblos and surrounding Spanish communities for more than 300 years.

Left: **Ruins of the mission at Quarai. (Detail of MNM #6653)**
Above: **Interior of what was once the mission church at Quarai. (MNM #87728)**

CHAPTER 3

COLONIAL SANTA FE

On September 13, 1692, Don Diego de Vargas led a force of 200 back into Santa Fe, which their countrymen had been forced to abandon a dozen years earlier, and reclaimed the region for Spain and the Catholic Church. Pacifying the rest of the province was more difficult. During the next few years de Vargas engaged in a bloody struggle to subdue outlying pueblos, where resistance to renewed Spanish control remained strong. By 1697 life for the *reconquistadores* had settled down except for periodic raids by Navajo and Plains Indians that lasted into the late nineteenth century. Settlers now turned their attention to daily living.

The Spanish brought with them a number of innovations that radically enhanced life in this barren land. Along with their guns and armor, they carried metal farming implements, saws, axes, knives, chisels, pots, and pans. They used readily available materials and, with ingenuity, creativity, and resourcefulness, developed an elemental, organic, simple way of life in tune with the seasons and shaped by a deep religious faith. They formed a community centered on the church and the needs of their families. And as Spanish colonial life evolved, it demonstrated the qualities that would characterize it for the next 300 years: durability, stability, simplicity, and harmony.

The settlements that developed in northern New Mexico were centered on plazas, *acequias*, and a communal economy. Settlers farmed individual plots, grazed sheep on communally held pastures, and gathered wood from communally held forests. Families were bound to each other through their arrangement of water rights; a barter economy; and a common need for entertainment, help in building, tending flocks and crops, caring for the sick and infirm, and burying the dead.

Left: **Original adobe homes were built to the street line.** Above: **Painting by B.J.O. Nordfeldt. (MNM #31806)**

ACEQUIAS

Agua es vida. Every New Mexican understood that in this arid landscape water was life. Few things better dramatize that fact than the enormous, locally controlled network of hand-dug irrigation ditches – called *acequias* – that thread their way throughout the mountain villages and distribute rain and snowmelt to small farmers in the valleys and towns. The concept of directing water through ditches was originally introduced to Spain by the Moors. It is estimated that at one time there were between 800 and 1,200 distinct ditch systems watering countless small plots of *chile*, beans, corn, squash, melons, orchards, and alfalfa fields throughout New Mexico. *Acequias* were among the first civic works undertaken by the colonists, who expanded upon the simpler irrigation systems the Pueblos had been using for centuries.

In remote villages the *acequia* association served as the central civic institution and over time evolved into a small yet powerful governmental body. Water rights were (and remain) a precious commodity, and the decentralized system familiar throughout New Mexico has allowed rural residents to maintain some measure of local control and prevent the manipulation of water by stronger forces. This has enabled some

norteños to continue to live a traditional way of life. While many villages have lost their common pastures and woodlands, they still have their water.

Soon after the Spanish colonists settled in Santa Fe, they dug the Acequia Madre, or Mother Ditch, as required by the Laws of the Indies. It ran south seven miles from Upper Canyon Road to Agua Fría Village and at one time had as many as thirty-eight branches that watered fields and orchards throughout the city. Today that number has been reduced to just four that are still somewhat active: Acequia Madre, Acequia Llano, Acequia Murilla, and Acequia Cerro Gordo. By the late nineteenth century a public utility took control of the city's water resources to provide service to all residents, and only recently has the ditch association regained the right to a weekly flow in the Acequia Madre.

New Mexicans remain deeply connected to their *acequias*. One of the traditions that mark the change of seasons is the annual spring cleaning of the ditches, when all stakeholders turn out with rakes and shovels to clear them of leaves, fallen branches, and other debris that has collected since the end of the last irrigation season.

Opposite Page: **The Acequia Madre ran south seven miles from Upper Canyon Road to Agua Fría Village. (Detail of MNM #11047)**

Left: **Adobe bricks have always been made by hand in wooden forms.** (MNM #40620)
Right: **Adobe plastering was traditionally a family and communal project.** (MNM #66644)

was a combination of what was practiced in Mexico and what they learned from the Pueblo Indians. Houses had small rooms built to a width dictated by the length of available roof beams (*vigas*) that were made from the peeled trunks of ponderosa pines set approximately two feet apart. On top of the *vigas* the Spanish placed rows of peeled saplings or split cedar branches, called *latillas*, over which they laid a bed of willow branches topped with layers of straw or *chamisa*, clay, and dirt. Water and snowmelt drained from this earthen roof through *canales* cut from hollowed logs. They then plastered the walls inside and out with a coat of mud mixed with straw.

As families grew and the need arose, the Spanish settlers, like their Pueblo neighbors, scratched out the footprint of a new room and added it to the existing structure. There were no interior hallways connecting rooms; each had its own door to the outside. These rows of rooms began to form compounds, many of them in a south-facing *L* or *U* shape that created a little *placita,* which absorbed the winter sun and provided an outdoor work space.

BUILDING

Nothing characterizes Santa Fe more than its distinctive adobe homes. Originally these were small, simple structures rooted in nature, prescribed by necessity, shaped by the climate, and marked by resourcefulness. They exhibited a sense of humility and a lack of pretension. Out of the materials that were easily gathered — stone, mud, straw, brush, and trees — the early settlers fashioned

adequate shelters for their families.

The Spanish brought with them a simple wooden form with which they turned a mixture of mud and straw into uniform sun-dried adobe bricks. These were then laid up with mud mortar into walls. This was a variation on the Pueblo tradition of making walls of rough hand-formed mud blocks and puddled adobe. The rest of Spanish home-building technology

Above: **A shepherd's bed above a corner fireplace was a warm and cozy place to sleep.**

FIREPLACES AND CHIMNEYS

The Spanish made existence indoors measurably more comfortable than that known by the Pueblo Indians with the introduction of the corner (or *kiva*) fireplace and a chimney to draw out the smoke. The Pueblo Indians had traditionally lived with open fires in their rooms and exhausted the smoke through a hatch in the roof. The chimney gave the Spanish the luxury of smoke-free interiors and allowed them to cook indoors, while the Indians had mainly cooked over open fires outside. A built-in platform next to and above the fireplace, known as a shepherd's bed, provided a warm and cozy place to sleep.

Above: **Plastering a corner fireplace. (MNM #61635)**

CANALES

The *canale* was a critical feature of the local adobe architecture. Despite a relatively low annual precipitation, Santa Fe gets its share of rain and snow. With flat roofs sheathed only in layers of brush, clay, and dirt, getting the moisture off the roof before it could seep into the rooms below was a perpetual problem. The answer was the *canale*, a drain spout first fashioned from hollowed-out tree trunks. Over time, the *canale* of old has evolved into a unique design element. Today you can still find a few made from logs, but more commonly they are created in all sorts of geometric designs, cut from tin, lined with copper, and even welded into steel gargoyles.

ZAGUANS

The houses of the wealthy were often built in the *hacienda* style. Within the city these houses were constructed to the property line for purposes of defense. Four rows of rooms sheltered by *portales* formed a square to enclose an open *placita* in a house form long popular in North Africa and southern and central Spain. The windows, doors, and *portales* faced inward toward the courtyard with sole access through a *zaguán* – a pair of heavy gates wide enough to permit the passage of wagons and horses. A smaller gate through which individuals could easily pass in and out of the courtyard was cut into one of the larger doors. This made a protective enclosure for the extended family and its livestock. The walls of the rooms that faced the outside served as further protection. They were three or more feet thick, stood twelve to fourteen feet high, and were topped with a parapet that extended several feet above the finished roof to serve as a breastwork in the event of an attack. A large *hacienda* located some distance from town might have *torreones*, or towers, at its four corners for additional defense.

Above: **A *zaguán* gate at the Vigil residence on Alto Street. (Detail of MNM #43372)**

WINDOWS

Windows in simple colonial homes remained small and were often guarded with a grille of vertical poles. If not glazed with sheets of mica or selenite, they were closed with a pair of shutters that swung on wooden pintle hinges, as did doors before metal hinges were available.

FAITH
AND FAMILY

The family and the church were the core of colonial
life. Most people lived a subsistence existence in
which they provided for their own needs. They built
their own houses, grew their own food, raised their
own animals, made their own clothing, and crafted
their own furniture and utensils. Central to daily living
was their Catholic faith. Some even maintained
their own chapel or altar, and often the only decoration in a simple colonial home was a religious
object, such as a cross, a carved *santo*, or some
representation of the Virgin of Guadalupe. Life's
significant events were celebrated through the
church, and the passage of time was marked by
religious holidays.

Left: **Husking corn on a simple northern
New Mexico homestead. (MNM #4219)**
Right: **San Miguel Church, considered the
oldest church in the country.**

FOOD PRODUCTION AND PREPARATION

Under the Laws of the Indies, each colonist was granted rights to communal pastures and forests as well as land for farming. More than three-quarters of the land within the area of the town was devoted to irrigated plots that were tilled with wooden plows and large hoes. When it came to food production and preservation, the Spanish settlers took their lead from the Pueblo Indians and subsisted largely on a diet of beans, corn, squash, and *chile*. The Spanish introduced the cultivation of wheat, which they ground into flour and baked into bread in a beehive-shaped adobe oven called an *horno*. Corn was ground in a stone *metate*, mixed with water into small balls of dough, patted or rolled flat, and cooked on an iron *comal* into *tortillas*, a staple brought north from Mexico. Like their Pueblo neighbors, the Spanish ate corn mush, often spiced with *chile* peppers, at virtually every meal. Rather than sitting on chairs at a table (few houses enjoyed such luxuries), settlers ate from a plate held on their knees using a spoon (there were no knives and forks) or a *tortilla*.

The Spanish also brought with them fruit trees and melons and all manner of domestic livestock, including horses, cattle, donkeys, sheep, goats, and chickens. This in turn led to the development of corrals enclosed by coyote fences made of vertical cedar saplings within which Spanish settlers kept their stock safe from predators.

Top: **Threshing wheat with goats. (MNM #9059)** Bottom: **Winnowing beans. (Detail of MNM #31499)**

Top: **Baking bread.**
(Detail of MNM #69106)
Bottom: *Chile* **harvest.**
(Detail of MNM #31507)

CUSTOMS

The Catholic Church was the center of the community, and life revolved around annual religious celebrations, church rituals, feast days of patron saints, baptisms, weddings, and funerals. Among the more important religious events in Santa Fe and surrounding villages was the annual procession of Corpus Christi.

Weddings were joyous affairs in remote New Mexican villages. While marriage vows were exchanged at the church, parents waited in the house of the bride. The wedding party was then escorted through the streets to the strains of a violin and guitar accompanied by shouts and shots fired into the air. A short distance from the house, the bride and groom were met by a shower of tears and kisses from parents, relatives, and friends, who fell in and joined the march to where a banquet had been prepared. They sang and danced all afternoon before going home to prepare for the wedding dance that night at the village hall, where the walls were festooned with mirrors to give it an elegant appearance. By dawn the wedding couple returned to the home of the bride to receive the blessings of the parents and older relatives before embarking on their life together.

Left: **Wedding procession. (MNM #12034)** Above: **Corpus Christi Procession. (MNM #87047)**

COLONIAL ARTS

Forced by isolation to fend for themselves and to fashion what they needed out of what little was available, colonial New Mexicans wove their own cloth, made their own tools and household items, crafted their own furnishings, and carved and painted their own religious articles. And from their isolation sprang a unique folk culture and style that reached a level of artistic distinction. The area became known for religious icons, such as *santos*, *bultos*, *retablos*, crosses, and representations of the Virgin of Guadalupe in all forms; finely crafted *colcha* needlework; and beautiful weavings in soft, natural colors. They used native pine boards to build chests, chairs, *trasteros*, and doors that were both simple and pleasing in their proportions. They relieved the blank appearance of the pieces with elaborate chip carving and geometric designs.

Left: **Weaver. (MNM #6918)**
Right: ***St. Michael* by Molleno.**
(Museum of Spanish Colonial Art #1954.11)

The religious folk art reflected its new surroundings. Traditional symbols of widely accepted iconography became particularly localized. One early example is the *retablo* (far left) of Joseph leading a donkey carrying Mary on their way to Bethlehem. The local version shows them passing a hollyhock (a very beautiful local flower) with a roadrunner (New Mexico's official bird) perched on top. Another *retablo* (left) shows Saint Raphael, the patron saint of travelers, holding a large whiskered catfish, which is a common local fish.

Opposite Page Left: *Flight into Egypt* by Pedro Antonio Fresquís. (Museum of Spanish Colonial Art 1965.10)
Opposite Page Right: *Saint Raphael* by Bernardo Miera y Pacheco. (Museum of Spanish Colonial Art 1954.77)
Right: *Santero* José Dolores López. (MNM #94470)

COLONIAL FURNITURE

At least seven carpenters traveled north with Oñate in 1598, each equipped with tool kits including axes, chisels, augers, planes, adzes, hammers, and even some nails. Nevertheless, furniture in Colonial New Mexico remained scarce, even in the homes of the wealthy. Seating in most homes was on a simple blanket-covered *colchón*, or mattress, that was rolled up during the day and set against the wall in a style imported from Moorish Spain. At night these mattresses were unrolled for sleeping. A few people owned chairs, and most had a trunk (originally made of rawhide and later pine) to store clothes and family valuables. Some had pine chests that held grain.

Opposite Page: **Early Colonial seating was often just a simple bench.**
Left: *Trasteros* **were freestanding cupboards used to hold clothes and household goods.**
Above: **Chests were often carved with elaborate geometric patterns.**

As time went on the most common types of furniture were benches, chairs, chests, *trasteros* (cupboards), and tables, plus built-in cupboards called *alacenas*. Many of their parts – particularly spindles – were decorated with symbols that came from the Pueblo Indians, such as lightning bolts, rain clouds, mountain profiles, and step designs. Others bore Spanish figures, such as rosettes, scallops, flowers, and cruciforms. Some were carved with bullet, basket weave, and rope designs, while others were decorated with geometric patterns. Among the rich as well as the poor, homes were sparsely decorated, and almost all objects had utilitarian value.

Right: **This enormous chest was built to hold wheat, corn, and other grains and flours.**

Left: **This built-in wall cupboard called an *alacena* is richly decorated with different spindles and geometric carvings.**

THE AMERICANIZATION OF SANTA FE

THE AMERICANIZATION OF SANTA FE ACTUALLY BEGAN IN 1821, WHEN MEXICO WON ITS INDEPENDENCE FROM SPAIN AND NEW MEXICO BECAME THE NORTHERN-MOST PROVINCE OF THE NEW REPUBLIC OF MEXICO. AT THAT TIME FEW COMMUNITIES HAD BEEN AS ISOLATED AS THOSE OF NORTHERN NEW MEXICO, HEMMED IN BY MOUNTAINS, DESERTS, AND MARAUDING PLAINS INDIANS, DEPENDENT ON PRIMITIVE WHEELED TRANSPORT, AND WITHOUT NAVIGABLE RIVERS. THE REGION'S GEOGRAPHIC SEPARATION BRED SOCIAL AND CULTURAL INSULARITY. FOR TWO CENTURIES THE SPANISH KEPT A TIGHT REIN ON NEW MEXICO'S BORDERS, FURTHER LIMITING OUTSIDE INFLUENCES ON SANTA FE. THE ONLY OPEN TRADE ROUTE WAS SOUTH ALONG THE CAMINO REAL TO THE TRADING CENTER OF CHIHUAHUA AND ON TO THE ADMINISTRATIVE CAPITAL IN MEXICO CITY.

Third Order of Saint Francis. These *hermanos* assumed responsibility for religious instruction and sustained the Catholic Church in many areas during the next thirty or forty years. They built their own windowless, adobe-brick chapels, called *moradas*. They decorated them with their own hand-crafted religious figures. And they practiced their own rituals in their own way, particularly around Holy Week, when they carried heavy wooden crosses and reenacted the Passion with devout members portraying Christ and his disciples.

Mexican control brought significant changes to Santa Fe. A new allegiance to Mexico was celebrated with an elaborate fiesta each Sixteenth of September, Mexico's independence day. This annual celebration started in the late 1820s and continued until the start of American occupation in 1846. The new Mexican government provided New Mexicans with their first taste of participatory democracy, as local delegates were elected to represent the province at the National Congress in Mexico City. And Mexican officials instituted a new social order that outlawed the old caste system, treated everyone equally before the law, and by the 1830s abolished slavery. Henceforth no one was to be classified by his racial origins, and all New Mexicans proudly called themselves *ciudadanos Mejicanos*, or citizens of Mexico.

Above: **Northern New Mexico Morada**. Right: **The northern New Mexico village of Chimayó. (MNM #13766)**

It took several months to make the round-trip in the creaking ox carts of the day with their screeching wooden axles and cumbersome wheels made from slices of enormous tree trunks. Most of the northbound cargo was consigned to resupplying the Franciscans in the scattered Pueblo missions, and what few consumer goods these wagon trains brought to Santa Fe fetched prices far beyond the means of most local people.

The vast distances and geographic remoteness that characterized all of New Mexico left the northern settlements particularly secluded. Santa Feans passed their simple lives focused on their family relations and religious beliefs. After gaining its independence from Spain, the Mexican government expelled the last few Spanish priests, and local people became more reliant upon themselves to fulfill their religious needs. Some built altars inside their homes or stand-alone chapels nearby. Some carved and painted their own *santos*, crosses, and other objects of worship.

And some of the faithful turned to the Penitente Brotherhood, a confraternity of lay practitioners that grew out of the

MEXICAN SANTA FE

By 1821 Mexico City had been the center of the regional empire for 200 years. It was there that the Spanish, already a blend of Arab, African, and other European peoples, added the blood of Mexican Indians to the mix. Later came further intermarriage with Pueblo and Plains Indians. As a consequence, Santa Fe's population, while not large, was extremely broad in its ethnic makeup. New Mexico became a land of great *mestizo* heritage whose legacy is visible today in customs, religion, food, music, dress, and art, much of it rooted in old Mexico.

In Santa Fe the music derived from the simple tunes of Mexico, played on the guitar, violin, and bass, still a common sound. With the twentieth-century addition of brass instruments, the original ensemble evolved into the now-familiar *mariachi* music, which is performed today at many New Mexican celebrations. The Mexican contribution to local cuisine includes

This Page: **Santa Fe Fiesta dancer. (MNM #117707)** Opposite Page Bottom Left: ***Los Travadores*, Santa Fe Fiesta. (Detail of MNM #44429)** Opposite Page Top Right: **Santa Fe Fiesta. (Detail of MNM #117848)**

tomatoes, *chile*, corn, *tortillas*, and chocolate, along with such favorite dishes as *burritos*, *tamales*, and *enchiladas*. The Mexican influence on clothing is seen during Fiestas when women wear the Mexican folk costume of wide skirts and peasant blouses. And the *mariachi* costume grew out of the elegant trappings of the *charro*, which included a broad-brimmed *sombrero* trimmed in silver or gold thread, short jacket with silver buttons, and tight trousers with the outside seams decorated with a row of silver buttons that ran from the hip to the hem. For everyday wear, native Santa Fe women never ventured out without a *rebozo*, a large Mexican-style shawl that served many purposes, from apron to head covering.

Significant among the many things that made their way north from Mexico is the Virgin of Guadalupe. This indigenous religious figure is the patron saint of the poor. According to legend, she first appeared as an apparition to Juan Diego, a Mexican Indian, on December 9, 1531. She was appropriated by the Spanish in their efforts at Native conversion. In 1810, at the start of the Mexican war for independence, Don Miguel Hildago y Costilla adopted her as the embodiment of *mestizo* liberation. Today Nuestra Señora de Guadalupe remains the most powerful religious symbol in Santa Fe and northern New Mexico.

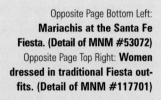

Opposite Page Bottom Left: **Mariachis at the Santa Fe Fiesta. (Detail of MNM #53072)** Opposite Page Top Right: **Women dressed in traditional Fiesta outfits. (Detail of MNM #117701)**

Wagon ruts along the Santa Fe Trail. (MNM #12845)

OPENING THE SANTA FE TRAIL

From the last quarter of the eighteenth century, French and Anglo traders from St. Louis and points east had cast a covetous eye on the profits they dreamed could be earned from trading with the Spanish. But most of those who managed to make it across the international border in present-day Kansas were arrested, imprisoned in Santa Fe, and stripped of their possessions. Some of the least lucky ones were shipped south to Chihuahua to toil in the mines, sometimes for years. But with the change from Spanish to Mexican control, this old xenophobia soon melted away. Mexican policies opened the

territory to trade from the American East. New Mexicans welcomed visitors who made the 800-mile trek from the Missouri River to exchange pots, pans, and calico cloth for silver, gold, and furs. And the age of the Santa Fe Trail was born.

The first to make a successful trading expedition to Santa Fe was a Missouri entrepreneur named Captain William Becknell, who is generally considered the father of the Santa Fe Trail. Having heard rumors of a change in government in Santa Fe, he loaded a train of pack mules with trade goods and struck out for the Rocky

Mountains, not sure what he would encounter. Ten weeks out of Arrow Rock, Missouri, his party met a group of Mexican soldiers in eastern New Mexico who gave him a warm welcome, though neither side could speak the other's language. Becknell arrived in Santa Fe to much fanfare on November 16, 1822, sold his goods in a matter of days, and within a month was on his way back to Missouri to broadcast his good fortune.

Becknell is reported to have made a 2,000 percent profit on his initial $3,000 in trade goods. On that first trip he probably

Wagons on the Santa Fe Trail. (MNM #12014)

For the next twenty-five years countless others took Becknell's advice and became richer for their efforts. Two years after Becknell's journey a company of eighty-one men and twenty-five wagons made the trip from Franklin, Missouri, and back in just over four months and turned an investment of $30,000 in merchandise into $180,000 in precious metals and another $10,000 in furs.

Wagon trains loaded with shiny tools, store-bought clothes, and bright cloth caused great anticipation as they rumbled over Glorieta Pass and down what's now known as the Old Santa Fe Trail and into the Santa Fe Plaza. Goods were stored in buildings along the Plaza's east side, which served as the customs house, before being distributed to wholesale and retail merchants. This trade prompted the construction of large mercantile buildings along the south and west sides of the Plaza that served as both retail stores and wholesale warehouses. The Missouri traders introduced long-isolated Santa Feans to a whole new world. Easterners were met by a warm and generous population who generally offered unlimited hospitality to strangers and readily shared what little they had with no demand or expectation of compensation.

By the time the U.S. Army took control of the territory in 1846, the value of trade on the Trail topped $1.7 million a year. It continued to grow, and in the last year of the Civil War almost 4,500 wagon trains made the trip to Santa Fe, which had become the central distribution center for all of New Mexico and Arizona.

Above: *The End of the Trail* by Gerald Cassidy. (MNM #6977)
Right: **A wagon train at the end of the Santa Fe Trail on San Francisco Street.** (MNM #11329)

carried a wide variety of fabrics, from broad-cloth to muslin, drills, prints, taffeta, calico, linen, and velveteen, along with buttons and buckles, needles, thread, and knitting needles; razors and razor strops; pots, pans, and coffee mills; and shovels, hoes, axes, and knives. He was an immediate hit and advised other prospective traders to bring nothing but quality goods, as the residents of Santa Fe had access only to the remains of old stock that had been brought up from Mexico, much of it damaged. He told them that they would find plenty of mules and money at the end of their trip and that they could expect to be paid whatever they asked, provided that what they offered met their customers' needs or fancies.

Above: **Engraving of Fort Marcy.** (MNM #1738)

SANTA FE UNDER AMERICAN RULE

In 1846 General Stephen Watts Kearny led a troop of cavalry into Santa Fe and claimed the entire New Mexican territory for the United States as a spoil of its imperialist war against Mexico. The tale of this "bloodless conquest" is one of history's myths. Many local people deeply resented the occupation, the change of their laws and language, foreign rule, and the threat of land seizures. Rebellion broke out in Taos, where Governor Charles Bent was killed, and bloody retaliation by U.S. forces took the lives of many Mexicans and Native Americans.

When the army took over in Santa Fe, the city had 4,500 residents. Physically it had changed little in 200 years. Adobe was still the favored building material. *Vigas*, *canales*, and corbels remained typical elements of the flat-roof earthen buildings. Churches were among the few structures that stood more than one story high. Most buildings had floors of hardened adobe, with the single exception of the Plaza-area store owned by John Scolly, which had a floor of wooden planks. The army brought new tools, materials, and building techniques that created rapid change in this dusty provincial outpost within a few short decades. The military imported the region's first power saw, which produced dimensioned lumber that enabled the development of the Territorial style of architecture marked by square *portal* posts and Greek Revival pediments over doors and windows.

For the next thirty years trade over the Santa Fe Trail thrived as Missouri drovers brought everything and anything imaginable from Independence and points east, including factory-made brick, tin roof panels, plate glass, nails, clothes and shoes, bolts of cloth, even pianos and the region's first printing press. Eastern – and military – influences inspired the spread of New England and Midwestern housing designs and details.

Left: **Officers' quarters,
Fort Marcy. (MNM #1695)**
Below: **Bakery, Fort Marcy.
(MNM #1711)**

These included pitched roofs, brick walls and roofline coping, picket fences, and multipaned factory-made windows. Several German-Jewish sutlers who came to supply the U.S. Army stayed to service Santa Fe, the outlying farming villages, and the entire territory. Bishop (later Archbishop) Jean Baptiste Lamy arrived in 1851 with a wealth of grand plans to improve the health, education, and welfare of his new flock, and left a legacy of churches, schools, and hospitals, many built in the Gothic, Romanesque Revival, and Second Empire styles then popular in his native France.

Above: **San Fransico Street, looking toward the Cathedral. (MNM #15325)**

TERRITORIAL STYLE

The U.S. Army brought with it the Territorial style, which incorporated simple elements of the Greek Revival style whose popularity had peaked back East a decade earlier. Buildings in the downtown area, though made of adobe, were adorned with square *portal* posts and brick coping details that topped roof parapets. East San Francisco Street leading up to the Cathedral (left), formally lined with a series of simple adobe Spanish/Pueblo vernacular buildings, now took on the new style. The Hotel Capital (right) sported a two-story porch with square railing spindles. Even the Palace of the Governors (below) was remodeled in the new Territorial style with a *portal* of square posts.

Above: **Hotel Capital.**
(MNM #56237)
Left: **Palace of the**
Governors with a
Territorial style *portal*.
(MNM #9099)

TERRITORIAL DETAILS

Below: **The Borrego House is a classic Territorial style building.(MNM #191923)**
Opposite Page: **Territorial details introduced more than 150 years ago are still visible in Santa Fe today.**

A Spanish deed shows that the Rafael Borrego House (below) on Canyon Road dates back to 1753. By the late nineteenth century it had been remodeled in the Territorial style. The posts of the long *portal* are square, as are the white pickets that form the fence. The windows are framed in wide moldings and flanked by shutters. A simple triangular pediment tops the front door, and brick coping runs along the top of the *portal*.

Once the army set up New Mexico's first sawmill in the Santa Fe Canyon at the top of Canyon Road, dimensioned lumber became widely available, and residences such as the Borrego House began to adopt the new design elements. Rectangular sawn beams replaced round log ceiling *vigas*. Windows were set to the outside face of adobe walls and framed with simple casings and lintels. As factory-made materials became more available, builders cut larger openings into older adobe walls and filled

them with double-hung windows with multiple panes. They flanked doors with side windows and transoms, and an elaborate entryway became a building's most prominent feature. Moldings meant to simulate Greek column capitals replaced corbels. Brick roof copings in a variety of patterns, which imitated Greek dentils, were added to the tops of adobe walls. This created a dash of design, while slowing the erosion of the mud-brick parapets.

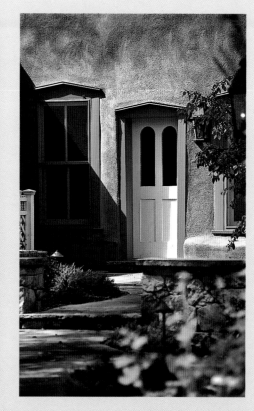

Opposite Page: **Brick copings in a variety of patterns.** Above: **The Felipe Delgado house. (Detail of MNM #191925)** Left: **Territorial-style windows.**

watchful eye of the U.S. Army, Easterners had been trying to cleanse the city of its architectural heritage. Most failed to see much charm in the low houses built of mud. Several months after the railroad connected Santa Fe to the outside world, President Rutherford B. Hayes came on an inspection trip accompanied by General William Tecumseh Sherman, who exhorted the local citizens to improve their lands and develop their vast resources before the Yankees came and did it for them. He urged them to get rid of their burros and goats and expressed the hope that in ten more years he wouldn't see another adobe house in the entire Territory. "I want to see you learn to make them of brick, with slanting roofs," he said. "Yankees don't like flat roofs, nor roofs of dirt." While over the next twenty years the town did attract Yankee arrivals and some of the houses were in fact built of brick with slanted roofs, most of the local population ignored the general's admonition and continued to build as it always had.

Around the Plaza, however, many of the large adobe buildings, some of which had taken on Territorial style characteristics earlier, were now replaced by even larger Victorian ones. These were built of brick and embellished with popular contemporary architectural details, including pressed-tin ceilings, cast-iron columns and storefronts, fancy roof brackets and cornices, heavy window eyebrows, elaborate trim and molding, and ornately carved doors.

In 1888 attorney Thomas B. Catron (leader of the notorious Santa Fe Ring, a group of powerful ranchers, businessmen, and

VICTORIAN SANTA FE

By 1863 the Eastern Division of the Union Pacific Railway began laying track west from Kansas City, and for the next fifteen years the Santa Fe Trail grew shorter as the railroad pushed farther west. On February 9, 1880, Santa Fe was finally connected to the Atchison, Topeka, and Santa Fe Railway by an eighteen-mile spur from the mainline station at Lamy, and the old color and clamor of the days of the Trail came to an end.

The coming of the railroad coincided with New Mexico's quest for national acceptance and the push for statehood. In order to appear like any typical American town, Santa Fe embraced the flood of imported manufactured building products shipped in from the East that spawned the construction of many buildings in the Victorian, Italianate, and Railroad Commercial styles popular elsewhere.

Since first moving to Santa Fe under the

Above: **Preparation for driving the first spike, Santa Fe Central Railway. (MNM #14193)**
Right: **Santa Fe railroad depot, ca. 1912. (Detail of MNM #66658)**

politicians that controlled virtually every aspect of the area's politics and economics) replaced a large, two-story Territorial building with a new $40,000 Italianate commercial one (right). The brick was manufactured at the state penitentiary south of town, and the building's façade displayed a pressed-tin cornice, deep roof brackets, and eye-browed windows.

By 1892 the southwest corner of the Plaza was anchored by the three-story Victorian Romanesque Claire Hotel (left), the height of late-nineteenth-century fashion and service. The twenty-six-room hotel was made of pressed brick and red sandstone. It boasted steam heat, hot and cold running water, and the Territory's first passenger elevator. Even the Palace of the Governors (below) was given a Victorian facelift, and the old Territorial *portal* was topped with a heavy balustrade with turned spindles.

Above: **Victorian Romanesque style Claire Hotel. (MNM #139208)**
Right: **Victorian style *portal*, Palace of the Governors. (MNM #49158)**

Above: **Italianate style Catron Building. (MNM #67593)**

French Second Empire style St. Francis Sanitorium. (MNM #67744)

French Second Empire style Palace Hotel. (MNM #10766)

A TRAINLOAD OF STYLES

By the early decades of the twentieth century, Santa Fe was littered with a hodgepodge of architectural styles. In an attempt to win congressional approval for statehood, it had tried to look like Anywhere, U.S.A., and had largely succeeded. Guadalupe Church had changed its appearance from northern New Mexico Mission to tall-steepled, white-picket-fence New England style. Politicians met in an imposing marble-and-granite Capitol with a grand columned portico and rotunda beneath a stained-glass dome that rivaled the best in the nation. Citizens banked at the Greek Revival First National Bank, while the county commission met in a Victorian courthouse. The shopping blocks were Railroad Italianate, several large homes were built in Queen Anne, much new housing was Bungalow style, the Catholic schools were French Second Empire, and the St. Francis Cathedral and Loretto Chapel were Romanesque Revival and Gothic. In many cases, the underlying building remained simple adobe to which were added imported details the owner may have considered fashionable. In others various embellishments were overlayed onto a single building to create a whole new vernacular style, even to the extent of painting a plastered wall to look like brick. As the city searched for an identity, some builders latched onto the Mission Revival style popular in the Los Angeles area in the late 1890s and brought back along the railroad by the hotel architects for the Fred Harvey Company. It was marked by arches, low-pitched roofs covered with or trimmed in Spanish tile, and curvilinear parapets and gables.

But none of these styles became dominant in Santa Fe, and all were far removed from the traditional culture and values. That left the city primed for a revival of its own indigenous Spanish/Pueblo look.

Above: **California Mission Revival style railroad depot. (MNM #104466)** Right: **California Mission Revival style De Vargas Hotel. (MNM #10786)**

Above: **Neo-Classical style Territorial Capitol. (Detail of MNM #10392)** Right: **Greek Revival style First National Bank, Santa Fe Plaza. (MNM #10640)**

Above: **Neo-Palladian style Nathan Salmon's Dry Goods Store. (MNM #61442)** Right: **Italianate style Commercial Hotel. (Detail of MNM #14033)**

Above: **Rustic Tudor style Santa Fe County Jail. (MNM #10248)**

Top: **California Mission Revival style Elks Club. (MNM #61366)**
Bottom: **California Mission Revival style Women's Board of Trade Library. (Detail of MNM #56603)**

Above: **Territorial Victorian style.**
Above Right: **Queen Anne style. (MNM #56846)** Right: **New England style Guadalupe Church. (MNM #10036)**

Left: **Mission Revival style.**
Bottom Left: **Dutch Colonial Revival style.** Bottom Right: **Bungalow style.**

CHAPTER 5

Left: *The Church at Santa Cruz* by **B.J.O. Nordfeldt. (MNM #111767)**
Bottom Right: **Artist John Sloan on a painting excursion. (MNM #28836)**

SAVING OLD SANTA FE

When Easterners started coming to Santa Fe by rail, many were not enamored of the primitive lifestyle they found. The simple adobe architecture and way of life often was viewed as backward, ignorant, and not equal to the level of advancement enjoyed by the places these people came from. Many sought to remake Santa Fe in their own image, with the styles and values they brought from someplace else.

One exception to this pattern of Americanization was exhibited by the artists and writers who stumbled into northern New Mexico just prior to the turn of the twentieth century. Some came for reasons of health when the clean mountain air of Santa Fe was gaining repute as an excellent curative for tuberculosis and other lung ailments. Others arrived in the midst of a search for an alternative way of life, running away from the growing standardization and industrialization then engulfing much of the urban United States. They were looking for uniqueness, sources of inspiration, and natural surroundings, all of which they found in abundance.

The Santa Fe they embraced had a drama all its own. It was original and primitive. It embodied an exotic combination of Spanish, Mexican, and Indian influences. It resounded with the cadence of foreign languages. Its raw, natural environment bespoke simplicity and humility. And beneath the surface ran the spirit of an amazing resourcefulness that had enabled the local population to survive in the harsh high desert for the previous three centuries.

Some days the sky was so blue that it evoked an almost aching intensity. Sometimes it filled with awe-inspiring cloud formations as if to announce the Second Coming. Some days the weather could cycle through all four seasons in one twenty-four-hour period. At 7,000 feet, the air was clear, the sky was radiant, and the light was brilliant.

The view alone, which could stretch a hundred miles, was open, unbound, and refreshing compared to what new arrivals had known back East. The vast expanse helped release the spirit from the structures and strictures of society. What first appeared drab was in fact rich in color. Instead of the endless green of the East and Midwest, the earth of the high Southwestern desert throbbed with brilliant reds, yellows, purples, and browns. The absence of a monochromatic vegetation cover revealed a whole new palette of possibilities.

There was a sparseness to the landscape that sharpened the definition of its randomness, its spontaneity, and its irregularity. Nothing was taken for granted. Nothing was overdone. There was a restraint that demanded a reaction from the spirit. And artists felt that immediately. The rawness of nature framed so vividly by the earth, the mountains, and the sky created a harmony and a balance known to few other places.

The adobe homes with their simple, organic elegance were in tune with and

Below: **New Mexico artists (left to right) Carlos Vierra, Gerald Cassidy, Theodore Van Soelen, Sheldon Parsons, and Datus Myers. (MNM #20786)**

at peace with the natural world around them. There was no artificial use of brilliant color, no gratuitous ornamentation — just a simple and subdued refinement that comes with age and tradition. The artists who settled in Santa Fe saw this. They saw the beauty in the common things of everyday living and the dignity of the humble life that accompanied it. In Santa Fe time had a different rhythm. There was no rush, there was no immediacy. *Mañana* was soon enough, and the day after tomorrow would do just as well.

The first great period for Santa Fe as an art colony coalesced in the early decades of the twentieth century when some of the most famous and highly regarded artists in the country came to settle. Officials at the Museum of New Mexico welcomed these newcomers and offered them free studio space, first at the Palace of the Governors and later at the new Fine Arts Museum, in a concerted effort to place Santa Fe squarely within the country's artistic consciousness. On the museum's twentieth anniversary, in a catalog that listed sixty-eight artists for the 1937 celebratory show, director Dr. Edgar Lee Hewett explained his long-standing policy to open the museum's alcoves to both eminent painters and unknown beginners, without fear or favor, and to "keep out of the way and give art a fair field."

Many of these artists enjoyed national and international reputations. They traveled far from Santa Fe to teach and exhibit but always anticipated their return. As they spread the word among their friends and associates living in other parts of the country, these artists became the city's first goodwill ambassadors. As such, they helped fuel a burgeoning tourist economy and created an allure the city still enjoys. When in town they worked hard at their craft and played hard at their newly crafted lives. They were active in Santa Fe civic life and were instrumental in preserving traditional Santa Fe architecture and in establishing what would become known as Santa Fe style.

Above: **Left to right, artists Marsden Hartley, Randall Davey, and John Sloan. (Detail of MNM #14232)**

RANDALL DAVEY (1887–1964)

Born in East Orange, New Jersey, Randall Davey studied art and architecture at Cornell University before moving to New York City in 1908 to study painting with Robert Henri. Later in his career he taught at the Chicago Art Institute, the Kansas City Art Institute, the Broadmoor Art Academy in Colorado Springs, and the University of New Mexico.

In 1919 he loaded up his 1912 Simplex, a ninety-horsepower, chain-driven open touring car, with friend and fellow painter John Sloan and their wives, and followed the advice of their mentor Henri to investigate the situation in Santa Fe. When they arrived on the Plaza they asked for directions to the then-two-year-old Fine Arts Museum. There they were greeted warmly, and museum officials provided them with studios to get started on their work

Below: **Randall Davey in the patio of the Palace of the Governors. (MNM #45189)**
Center: **Randall Davey residence. (Detail of MNM #191926)**
Opposite Page: **Randall Davey residence. (MNM #10518)**

right away. Davey and Sloan immediately made commitments to make Santa Fe their permanent residence.

In 1920 Davey bought the picturesque old mill and orchard that lay at the top of Canyon Road at the entrance to Santa Fe Canyon. The stone building, with sixteen-inch-thick walls, had been built by the U.S. Army in 1847 to house the territory's first circular saw, which provided milled lumber for the construction of Fort Marcy. Five years later the complex – which included the sawmill, a grist mill, two other houses, and a stable – was sold to well-known trader and trapper Ceran St. Vrain for $550. By the time Davey came along in 1920, the building had long been stripped of its milling machinery. He converted the former storeroom into his studio, where he cut large north-facing windows into the wall that overlooked the slopes of Santa Fe Canyon. He furnished the living quarters upstairs with English antiques and filled it with his paintings, murals, bronzes, sketches, photographs, journals, and other collectibles. Despite being a Western painter, he preferred nudes and horses to Native Americans, and many of his pieces are of his second wife and frequent model, Isabel Holt.

Davey died in a car accident in 1964 while en route to California. Since 1983 the home and surrounding 135 acres have been owned by the Audubon Society and are open to the public.

Opposite Page Top: **Studio, Randall Davey residence.** (MNM #191930)
Opposite Page Bottom: **Living room.** (MNM #191927)
This Page: **Mrs. Davey's dressing room.** (MNM #32104)

GERALD CASSIDY (1879–1934)

Below: **Gerald Cassidy with Native American children. (MNM #49203)**
Right: **Interior, Gerald Cassidy residence. (Detail of MNM #102205)**

Gerald Cassidy was born in Kentucky and raised in Cincinnati, the fourth of twelve children. His father was a builder, and Gerald was trained at the Institute of Mechanical Arts (later known as the Cincinnati Art Institute) under Frank Duveneck (whose other students included New Mexico artists Joseph Sharp and Walter Ufer). He became a noted lithographer in New York City before a case of pneumonia in 1898 worsened into a serious bout of tuberculosis and drove him to the healthier climate of Albuquerque.

He soon recovered in the clear, dry, Southwestern air and moved to Denver to pursue parallel paths of painting and commercial illustration. There he met and married author Ina Sizer, and by 1912 they settled in Santa Fe in a house on the 800 block of Galisteo Street, which she later recalled was still out in the country with no paved streets, no cars, and only a single sewer line.

Two years later they bought an old house at 924 Canyon Road (near the intersection with Acequia Madre). They enlarged and restored it with carved corbels and beams salvaged from the ruins of the colonial church at Nambé Pueblo. On one of these is inscribed, "The Lord Governor Don Juan Domingo built this church at his own expense in 1725." They also incorporated an altar screen painted by Bernardo Miera y Pacheco, one of the earliest known eighteenth-century New Mexican *santeros*. The Cassidys became founding members of Santa Fe's burgeoning art colony.

In 1915 Cassidy won a gold medal for one of a series of fifteen murals painted for the Panama-Pacific Exhibition in San Diego. Back in Santa Fe, he painted two majestic murals that initially hung in the lobby of the El Oñate Theater on the Plaza and now grace the lobby of the post office on South Federal Place. Other examples of his work are on display in La Fonda Hotel.

In February 1934, while working in a temporary studio on a mural project for the W.P.A., Cassidy was overcome by carbon monoxide fumes from a faulty gas heater. He died the next day.

Left: **Built-in cabinet with lightning-bolt grilles flanked by rope-carved posts, Gerald Cassidy residence. (MNM #102204)**
Right: *Portal* **with fireplace and daybed, Gerald Cassidy residence. (MNM #91637)**

SHELDON PARSONS (1866–1943)

Between 1895 and 1912, Sheldon Parsons was a successful New York City portrait painter of such national celebrities as President William McKinley and Susan B. Anthony. In 1913, following the death of his wife, he moved to Santa Fe with his twelve-year-old daughter, Sara (who ultimately became a noted artist in her own right), to help cure his tuberculosis. In 1918 he became the first director of the Museum of New Mexico.

Between 1924 and 1926, Parsons and his daughter bought three adjoining parcels on lower Cerro Gordo Road, where Parsons lived and painted until his death twenty years later. He renovated one of the existing structures and added a two-story wing that displayed the elements of the new Spanish/Pueblo Revival style: thick adobe walls, *vigas* projecting through the exterior walls, wooden *canales*, heavy wooden lintels, a long front *portal* between projecting walls, set back second-story rooms, and an irregular roof line. Inside were exposed *vigas*; exposed lintels over deep-set, multipaned windows; arched openings between rooms; a corner fireplace in every room; and *bancos* and *nichos* throughout. The home also displayed Parsons's personal touches, such as a painted staircase and banister and carved and painted doors.

Opposite Page Left: **Sheldon Parsons. (Detail of MNM #73941)** Opposite Page Right: **Arched openings between rooms, Parsons residence. (MNM #135232)** Above: **Studio, Parsons residence. (Detail of MNM #135233)**

Above: **Olive Rush painting a mural for the Santa Fe Public Library. (Detail of MNM #74015)** Right: **Olive Rush residence, Canyon road. (Detail of MNM #88049)**

OLIVE RUSH
(1873–1966)

Olive Rush was born in Fairmount, Indiana, to a Quaker family. At the age of seventeen she moved to Washington, D.C., where she studied at the Corcoran School of Art. After first visiting Santa Fe in 1914, she returned and bought a house at 630 Canyon Road in 1920. The home had been in the Sena-Rodriguez family for many generations and may even date to the colonial period. It was typical of the many houses purchased by painters and writers who flocked to the city in the early decades of the twentieth century, and it remains largely unchanged from its original appearance. Rush used the large, north-facing room as her studio, decorated the corner fireplace from floor to ceiling with her own fresco murals of Indian motifs, and furnished the space with her collection of Spanish and Native American artifacts.

In 1934 Rush was engaged by the W.P.A. to create a fresco for the foyer of the Santa Fe Public Library (now the state's History Museum). The mural is still there and reminds young readers, "Con buenos libros no estás solo" (With good books you are not alone). Other examples of her work may be seen inside the entrance to La Fonda Hotel.

Today her Canyon Road home still displays such original features as a wooden *canale* made from a hollowed log and carved Colonial-era style wooden shutters. Upon her death she willed the building and grounds to the Santa Fe Friends Meeting, and it is still used for weekly worship.

EUGENIE SHONNARD (1886–1978)

Eugenie Shonnard, a descendant of Francis Lewis, who signed the Declaration of Independence, was born in Yonkers, New York. Fragile and lonely as a child, she spent many hours with her beloved animals. She studied first at the New York School of Applied Design, where she discovered her love of clay and sculpture. In 1911, over the protests of her family and her doctor, she went to Paris, where she became strong and healthy while studying with Auguste Rodin. She arrived in Santa Fe in 1926, became enchanted by the Native Americans and surrounding landscape, and decided to stay.

The next year Shonnard's mother bought a home at 1411 Paseo de Peralta that had been built in 1890 by Philip Hesche, a master carpenter originally from Canada. She gave the house to her daughter as a wedding gift in 1934. It was a classical center-hall design with six rooms going from front to back. Each was comfortably furnished in middle-class Victoriana. The building was made of adobe brick with a hipped roof, and after it was finished the original owner added a porch with Victorian brackets and a bay window to the front. Shonnard turned a small barn out back into her studio and lived and worked on the property until her death at the age of ninety-one. She willed the lot and structures to the Museum of New Mexico Foundation.

Opposite Page: **Eugenie Shonnard.** (MNM #19129)
This Page: **Eugenie Shonnard residence.** (MNM #55149)

Opposite Page: **Eugenie Shonnard residence.**
(MNM #55144) Center: **(MNM #55152)**
Above: **(MNM #55151)**

CARLOS VIERRA
(1876–1937)

As the first professional Anglo artist to take up residence in Santa Fe, Carlos Vierra is considered the father of the city's art colony. He was born and raised in Moss Landing, California, the son of a Portuguese sailor. He studied at the Mark Hopkins Institute of Art in San Francisco, after which he signed aboard a wooden sailing ship for a six-month passage around Cape Horn to get to New York. There he found success as a cartoonist and marine painter. By 1904 he had developed serious lung problems. He moved to New Mexico, first to a small cabin along the Pecos River and later to Santa Fe, where he sought treatment at St. Vincent Sanatorium.

Once healthy again, Vierra opened a photography studio on the Plaza and spent much time photographing the mission churches in the surrounding pueblos. He became an early and vocal proponent of preserving the city's original architecture, and he sought ways to apply Pueblo and early Spanish building techniques and detailing to modern purposes. He played a vital role in developing the local Santa Fe Revival style and used those new-old design elements in the restoration of the Palace of the Governors. He then supervised every detail of the design and construction of the Fine Arts Museum, ensuring that the new Santa Fe Revival style conformed to all the particular principles he had so carefully formulated.

By 1918 Vierra had decided to establish his own historic district, something the city did not formalize for another forty years. His idea was to buy a large tract and sell lots only to builders who would erect homes that conformed to his notions of

Santa Fe style. To set the example he began construction on his own house at 1002 Old Pecos Trail (at the corner of Coronado Road) on land he bought from Frank Springer for $1. Springer, a member of the Board of Regents of the new Museum of New Mexico, had become Vierra's patron and fervent supporter some years earlier. Under restrictions in the deed, he granted Vierra and his wife title to the house and property until their deaths, whereupon they would revert to the Springer family. Vierra enlisted the help of architect Trent Thomas, a member of the Rapp and Rapp firm that had designed the Fine Arts Museum, who produced a painting of a two-story, step-back, Pueblo-style building that captured Vierra's concept for the perfect Spanish/Pueblo revival style residence. Vierra worked on building the house for the next three years and in the process inspired a young architect named John Gaw Meem, who had come to Santa Fe for his health in 1920 and would also leave a lasting mark on the architecture of the city.

More than any group that made Santa Fe its new home, the early artists, with their deep appreciation for the unique architectural forms, the local people, and their traditions and values, held back the tide of Americanization and modernization that tried to turn this city into just another typical American town.

Left: **Carlos Vierra painting a mural in Saint Francis Auditorium, Museum of Fine Arts.** (MNM #30856) Above: **Vierra residence.** (Detail of MNM #51922)

CHAPTER 6

CREATING A STYLE

As Santa Fe turned the corner from the nineteenth century into the twentieth, it found itself at a crossroads, its future uncertain. The half-century aspiration to become a state would not be realized for another dozen years. The Santa Fe Trail had been obsolete for two decades, and with it went the economic preeminence the city had once enjoyed. The railroad had reached the Southwest by 1878 but had bypassed Santa Fe, except for a small spur connecting the capital city with the main line.

That was enough to generate an initial burst of optimism among city merchants, who thought that even with this little spur line they would see renewed commercial activity. They built large, imposing Italianate commercial blocks around the Plaza and waited for business to come their way, as it had during the years of the Santa Fe Trail. Now, however, the commerce had shifted to the communities at the railroad's main stops in Las Vegas and Albuquerque, and Santa Fe was left isolated once again. The loss of business, combined with the withdrawal of the army and its purchasing power in the 1890s, sent the city into an economic and population decline that would last for three decades.

As city officials cast about for a new economic stimulus, they recognized the potential in tourism being made possible by rail traffic into the Southwest. Santa Fe was already successfully promoting itself as a health resort. It had also attracted a number of talented artists, writers, photographers, archaeologists, and architects. Many of them fell in love with the area and became the nucleus of a vibrant artistic and intellectual colony. This group had a markedly romantic view of their new home and became avid supporters of the traditional architecture and way of life. They led a movement to strip the city of recent Americanizing influences and return it to its authentic local roots. By 1912 *The Santa Fe New Mexican* was reminding its readers that visitors did not come to Santa Fe to "view Queen Anne cottages or factory chimneys," and letters to the editor advised Santa Feans to preserve their old traditions. Elected officials and business organizations got on board and began an effort to make Santa Fe the center of Southwestern tourism by developing a homogeneous Spanish/Pueblo architectural appearance that would come to be known as "Santa Fe style."

Above: **Construction of a new *portal*, Palace of the Governors. (Detail of MNM #13029)**

THE NEW-OLD SANTA FE STYLE

The effort to remake Santa Fe was influenced by the City Beautiful movement that swept across the country from 1900 to 1910. Cities were encouraged to refashion themselves in an attempt to bring beauty and order to the chaos created by the Industrial Age. In most places the movement focused on parks and boulevards, landscaping and street furniture, and monumental Neo-Classical Beaux-Arts-style public buildings surrounding grand civic plazas.

But not in Santa Fe. This was the only city where leaders chose instead to look inward and revive the indigenous architecture. Under the influence of the artists' community, the city planning commission, the chamber of commerce, and officials of the Museum of New Mexico, Santa Fe's leaders decided to create an architectural homogeneity based on preserving its own vernacular heritage. With its humble adobes, its narrow, twisting streets, its rich vocabulary of traditional architectural details, its Old World charm, and its unique urban form, Santa Fe recognized that it possessed the resources to stimulate tourism and economic recovery. In 1912 the planning board recommended bringing back the Spanish/Pueblo style, and soon the chamber of commerce began to promote Santa Fe as the "City Different."

Defining the elements of this revival style played itself out in the restoration of the Palace of the Governors, home to the Museum of New Mexico since its founding in 1909. The Palace was badly deteriorated and had been much altered over the centuries with the imposition of foreign styles. It had gone through an extensive Territorial remodeling, followed by a Victorian one. The goal now was to return it to the architecture of the period of its original construction.

In order to discover what that architecture entailed, members of the museum staff took countless photographs of old Santa Fe houses and the churches scattered among area pueblos and outlying villages. Then they sorted the images of traditional, vernacular details into consistent patterns, tossed aside what didn't fit, and developed a formal typology that would define the elements of this new Santa Fe style.

In November 1912 they unveiled their findings in an exhibit titled *New-Old Santa Fe*. It included enlargements of the photographs, the model for the restoration of the Palace of the Governors that demonstrated the application of the new style, a map of the city's ancient streets, and drawings of other Spanish/Pueblo-style buildings. The exhibit also discussed the issues of preserving both historic landmarks and humble adobes and how to hasten public recognition of Santa Fe as a tourism destination.

At that time, museum archaeologist and planning board member Sylvanus Morley, who had been an integral part of the Palace preservation effort, coined the term "Santa Fe style." And the city planning board recommended that no building permits be issued until it was satisfied that the architecture of the prospective project "will conform externally with the Santa Fe style."

In an effort to bring the buildings around the Plaza into compliance with the new style, Santa Fe's appointed tastemakers decided it was time to rip off the cast-iron store fronts, tear down the gingerbread trims, take off the Victorian brackets and dentils, discard the Grecian columns, and cover brick and stone façades with layers of brown cement stucco.

Above: **Model of the Palace of the Governors,** *New-Old Santa Fe* **exhibit. (MNM #6853)**

LOOKING
FOR ICONS

Architect Isaac Hamilton Rapp and his brother William enjoyed long and fruitful careers in Santa Fe, beginning in 1900 with the design for a new state Capitol of classical Greek proportions. A string of commissions soon followed that included schools, commercial buildings, a jail, a courthouse, a hospital, the governor's mansion, the Elks Club and Theater, Sunmount Sanatorium, and the Greek Revival First National Bank. But the design that would help set Santa Fe on a new architectural footing was the one they did for a supply store in Morley, Colorado. That design had been inspired by the San Esteban del Rey Mission Church at Acoma Pueblo, and its most prominent feature was the pair of towers that flanked its entrance. When Museum of New Mexico officials cast about for examples of what they wanted the New-Old Santa Fe style to look like, one design they latched onto was that of the Morley warehouse, and they included drawings of it in the 1912 exhibit.

When the Rapp brothers were selected to design the New Mexico Building for the 1915 Panama-California Exposition, they pulled out the Morley warehouse plans and built a replica in San Diego's Balboa Park. Two years later Rapp and Rapp designed the new Fine Arts Museum in Santa Fe, turning once again to the Morley/San Diego plans for a building whose details would become the quintessence of Santa Fe style.

Left: **San Esteban del Rey Mission Church, Acoma Pueblo. (MNM #53197)**

Above: **Rapp and Rapp rendering for Colorado Supply Company store, Morley, Colorado. (MNM #61210)**
Left: **New Mexico Building, Panama-California Exposition, San Diego, California. (MNM #6937)**

The twin towers so prominent on the museum's façade were soon replicated on several other important Santa Fe buildings, including La Fonda Hotel, El Oñate Theater, and the old federal building (opposite St. Francis Cathedral), which is now the Institute of American Indian Arts Museum, as well as private homes.

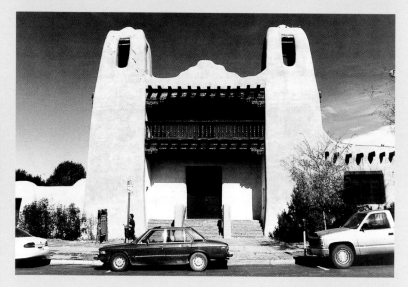

Above: **Private home.** Top Right: **Institute of American Indian Arts Museum.** Middle: **Saint Francis Auditorium (Fine Arts Museum).** Bottom Right: **Gross Kelly Warehouse.**

Left: **San Esteban del Rey Mission Church, Acoma Pueblo. (MNM #55492)** Above: **Museum of Fine Arts.**

Above: **Patio at the Museum of Fine Arts. (Detail of MNM #28886)**

MUSEUM OF FINE ARTS

The Museum of Fine Arts, built in 1917, embodies all the details that defined Santa Fe style. While actually constructed of brick and hollow tile, its basic form is drawn from the adobe mission church at Acoma Pueblo. The building surrounds an open patio, which is ringed by *portales* of heavy posts that support corbels and beams. The roof *vigas* protrude through the exterior walls. The beams and corbels are chip carved and painted in alternating patterns. A balcony with a carved railing similar to the choir loft at Acoma stretches across the rear of St. Francis Auditorium. Doors, windows, and radiator covers feature wooden grilles with geometric designs.

WILLIAM PENHALLOW HENDERSON

William Penhallow Henderson was one of the many Santa Fe artists who got involved in building in the Santa Fe Revival style. He had been a well-established painter in Chicago before moving to Santa Fe in 1916 so his wife, poet Alice Corbin, could recover from tuberculosis. After spending several months at Sunmount Sanitorium, the family moved into a modest home at the bottom of Camino del Monte Sol. Along with his flourishing painting career, Henderson formed a building company in 1925 and took on a variety of projects. He restored Sena Plaza and designed and built the Museum of Navajo Ceremonial Art (now called the Wheelwright Museum), as well as a number of private homes. One of his larger commissions was the complex of buildings on Garcia Street for Amelia Elizabeth White and her sister Martha, which now houses the School of American Research. Like so many builders working in this period, Henderson drew much of his inspiration from the mission churches (see below) and incorporated wooden details salvaged from buildings in mountain villages.

Henderson maintained a workshop where he produced chip-carved furniture, doors, and cabinets. One of his signatures was the way he gave texture to his surfaces with an adze.

Another was the rosette he carved into doors, beams, and cabinet fronts. He used the same motif in wall sconces and chandeliers he made from hammered tin.

He was also noted for his many built-ins. Early settlers who had little furniture flanked their corner fireplaces with built-in adobe *bancos* for seating, carved *nichos* into adobe walls to display religious objects, and set wooden *alacenas* (cupboards) into the walls for storage. Henderson used the same approach to furnish his houses by building wooden desks, dressing tables, closets, shelves, and cabinets into the walls.

Below: **Amelia White estate.**
(Detail of MNM #67893)

Above: *Portal*, Amelia White estate. (Detail of MNM #67888)

In 1924 Meem returned to Santa Fe, opened his own office, and became involved with the Society for the Restoration and Preservation of New Mexico Missions. Before the close of the decade he had mastered the use of traditional New Mexican materials and forms, directed the restoration of the mission church at Acoma Pueblo, completed a major remodeling of La Fonda Hotel, and designed homes for several prominent Santa Feans in his particular version of the Spanish/Pueblo Revival style. For the Laboratory of Anthropology he incorporated all the traditional details of a mission church — massive buttresses, post-and-beam *portal*, soft corners, and a choir loft. In the laboratory's library he used a low partition to create a corner fireplace in the middle of the room.

In the 1930s Meem and his associate Gordon Street developed a new style employing modern materials for large, public buildings while still projecting a regional idiom. Known as Territorial Revival, it drew on elements from the earlier Territorial style brought to Santa Fe by the U.S. Army. This new style first found expression in buildings within the Capitol complex and later made its way into private homes. Because of Meem's work and influence, it was later adopted by the city council as one of the two accepted regional styles (along with Spanish/Pueblo) allowed by the Historic Styles Ordinance in the historic zones.

JOHN GAW MEEM

Above: **Laboratory of Anthropology, Museum of New Mexico.**

After Isaac Hamilton Rapp, John Gaw Meem was the most significant architect to define Santa Fe's regional revival style. He was born in Brazil in 1894 to Episcopalian missionaries. He grew up speaking Portuguese and had a strong affinity for his Latin surroundings. He graduated from Virginia Military Institute with a degree in civil engineering, served in World War I, and came to Santa Fe in 1920 to recuperate from tuberculosis. He became friendly with artist Carlos Vierra, from whom he picked up a passion for Southwestern architecture. After regaining his health, he served a brief apprenticeship with an architect in Denver where he attended the evening program of the Beaux-Arts Institute of Design.

This Page: **Library at the Laboratory of Anthropology, Museum of New Mexico. (Detail of MNM #19647)**

FRANK APPLEGATE

Frank Applegate majored in architecture in college, and before moving to Santa Fe in 1921, he had been head of the Sculpture and Ceramics Department at the Trenton (New Jersey) School of Industrial Arts. He was an avid supporter of traditional local arts and was one of the founders of the Spanish Colonial Arts Society, which encouraged their revival. In 1927 he bought a tiny, old four-room adobe house near Camino del Monte Sol that had belonged to the de la Peña family and began an extensive remodeling and expansion. By the time the project was cut short by his death four years later, Applegate had already quadrupled the size of the original and turned it into a showplace of his fantasy of what constituted Spanish Colonial architecture.

Left: **The balconies and second-story railings, de la Peña house. (Detail of MNM #51186)**
Above: **A half-wall partition creates a corner fireplace, de la Peña house. (MNM #191928)**

CARICATURES OF TRADITION

From the outset, the attempt to preserve the indigenous architecture and the spirit of the local culture was compromised by other motives. Since the movement was conceived as a marketing tool to lure tourists, the new style basically appropriated superficial elements from the old traditions but never the values behind them. This new Santa Fe style lacked the essential qualities that informed the original: small, modest, low-profile, simple, functional, and free of gratuitous decoration.

In fact it was the opposite. The creators of Santa Fe style looked to the monumental gestures of the mission churches for their inspiration. They first incorporated them into the Fine Arts Museum, which became the exemplar. In successive decades this style morphed into adobe on steroids and public buildings and expensive homes grew bigger and bigger, more ornate, and more clichéd, their scale and form far removed from the simple homes of local people. The New-Old style spawned a huge market for architects and builders ready to exploit the possibilities of creating these new far-from-authentic replicas to meet the modern tastes of their rich clients. Some of the original details and specific elements may have been preserved, but lost is any connection to the traditional building forms and their relationship to the environment. The result has become a caricature of what once was an organic style that grew out of a sustainable and sensitive way of life.

Opposite Page Top: **The School for the Deaf. (MNM #50912)**
Opposite Page Bottom: **The Carlos Vierra residence was one of the first to break the pattern of the simple, one-story adobe house. (MNM #51927)** This Page: **The Inn at Loretto mimics the stepped-back forms of Taos Pueblo.**

SOUTHWEST INDIAN DETOURS

Once the Atchison, Topeka, and Santa Fe Railway penetrated the Southwest, tourists were lured into the unknown by romantic images of mountains, mesas, deserts, and Indians. This was a strange and lonely land, and travel was as harsh as the landscape. Conditions improved remarkably after entrepreneur Fred Harvey struck a deal to build restaurants and hotels along the route from Chicago to Los Angeles, which promised travelers comfortable lodging and excellent food. When Harvey took over management of Santa Fe's La Fonda Hotel in the late 1920s, *The Santa Fe New Mexican* reported with some measure of relief that finally the hotel would be providing "Harvey hotel service, Harvey hotel food, Harvey hotel standards."

A Harvey-owned Packard touring car met guests at the train in Lamy and brought them to the hotel on the Plaza. There the Harvey-owned Southwest Indian Detours offered excursions to

Left: **Harvey cars from La Fonda Hotel met tourists at the train depot in Lamy. (MNM #53651)**
Below: **Tourists enjoyed tea on the south** *portal* **of La Fonda Hotel. (MNM #54316)**

Below: **Harvey Indian Detours cars took tourists to the mountain village of Cordova. (MNM #44433)**
Right: **Tourists traveling in an Indian Detours car through the high mountain villages stopped in Truchas.(MNM #46949)**

nearby pueblos and archaeological ruins. Detour passengers were accompanied by college-educated, carefully screened female guides and hostesses who had taken crash courses in Southwestern art, geology, sociology, history, and architecture. They wore a uniform consisting of a long wool skirt, Indian velvet shirt, silver *concha* belt, and leather boots. The cars were driven by hand-picked young men, elegantly turned out in English-style riding boots, breeches, cowboy shirts, and the kind of ten-gallon hat favored by film star Tom Mix. The trips lasted one, two, or three days and took tourists to Native pueblos, Spanish villages, archaeological digs, and ruins. All meals and accommodations were arranged by the Fred Harvey Company.

All things Harvey are now gone, but tourism remains a mainstay of the Santa Fe economy, and people are still lured to the City Different and its unique charm.

CHAPTER 7

CONTEMPORARY SANTA FE

For 400 years travelers of every description have made their way to Santa Fe. Some have come in search of the Seven Cities of Gold, some to capture souls for the Catholic Church, some to escape the Inquisition in Spain and Mexico, some to scratch out a simple living, some to exploit the land for what it could produce in cattle, sheep, and minerals, some to trade manufactured goods for silver and furs, some to reclaim their health, some for the inspiration it lent their paintings, some for the money to be made servicing successive waves of wayfarers. Each incursion tampered with what it found, took what it could, and left its mark.

THE UNHISTORIC STYLE ORDINANCE

The New-Old Santa Fe style of 1912 was finally codified in 1957 in the Historic Styles Ordinance. It declared parts of the city, including the downtown and Eastside, "historic," and forced all new and remodeled buildings in those areas to conform to just two styles: the Spanish/Pueblo and the later-adopted Territorial Revival. The style police have tried to enforce a standardized physical appearance, but as in any American city, political and economic power often trump the law and anomalies arise without warning. After 1980 buildings in the downtown climbed above three stories, then four stories, then five stories and more, each design phonier than the one before and further from any relationship to traditional building and values. For centuries no structure in the Plaza area stood taller than the Cathedral. Today there are many, and the once clear view of the Jémez Mountains is obstructed by the massive Eldorado Hotel. The downtown has become what many refer to as an "adobe theme park" dedicated almost exclusively to serving the interests of tourists.

Left: **Graffiti on the construction barricade expressed local ire: "Coming Soon! 5 Story Fake Adobe Skyscraper," La Esquina building. (MNM #122817)**
Above: **The massive Eldorado Hotel blocks all views of the Jémez Mountains from downtown Santa Fe.**

MANSIONS CLIMB THE HILLS

Despite early-twentieth-century efforts by Anglo artists, the chamber of commerce, and many public officials to turn Santa Fe into a center for Southwest tourism, it remained through the 1970s a relatively sleepy, almost seedy town, far off the beaten path and unknown to most Americans. At the time few had heard of Santa Fe beyond mention in cowboy movies, and most thought a trip to New Mexico required a passport. That began to change after a ridiculous article in the May 1981 issue of *Esquire* put Santa Fe in the national spotlight in a distorted, untrue depiction that few who lived here could even recognize. Titled "The Right Place," it heralded Santa Fe as the new mecca for Porsche-driving, Gucci-wearing, coke-snorting New Age sophisticates in search of nirvana. The writer implored readers to spread the word among like-minded seekers — Santa Fe was IT!

That article unleashed a torrent of publicity, and this next "in place" attracted hordes of people who came not only to visit but also to buy their way into the new paradise. With that, Santa Fe became a haven for developers, and the city council enthusiastically supported a policy of unbridled growth. Fancy condominium complexes and gigantic private residences climbed the hillsides and spread out into the barren fringes of the county. The size and cost of homes exploded in direct proportion to the money looking for an outlet. Everything met the definition of the approved style with its conformist brown plaster, but lost in the rush was any true connection to the humble homes the new construction pretended to emulate.

SANTA FE SPRAWLS

As more and more people moved to Santa Fe, the city sprawled out in tightly packed, architecturally challenged subdivisions. The houses made a perfunctory nod to the traditional Santa Fe design aesthetic with their flat roofs and brown plastered walls. But the miles of faux adobe stucco cubes are mere caricatures of the early authentic architecture.

For the last fifty-plus years, Santa Fe has spread out from downtown and the historic Eastside in every direction. As the population swelled, motels, gas stations, restaurants, trailer courts, businesses, and stores followed in a straight line down Cerrillos Road, its main commercial artery. This line now stretches more than ten miles out to the southwest, anchored at the far end by shopping strips and malls occupied by all manner of national chain stores. Despite the generic nature of these big-box stores, in Santa Fe most sprout the requisite *viga* ends and are plastered in earth-tone stucco to make sure they are in keeping with the local style.

Right: **By the 1950s, Cerrillos Road had become Santa Fe's commercial strip. (Detail of MNM #29830)**

This Page: **Newly arrived chain stores play off the old Santa Fe style to make them appear to be long-time members of the community.**

MI CASA ES MI CASA

When the founding members of Santa Fe's original art colony arrrived at the turn of the twentieth century, they settled in among the local people. They learned their customs. They studied their history. They had an appreciation for the traditions that had informed their new home for hundreds of years. They were welcomed and treated with warmth and generosity.

This attitude of open hospitality prevailed through the 1970s. Today most new arrivals no longer take the time to discover where they are. Consequently, two worlds exist side by side and seldom meet. Many new-comers live behind high walls and locked iron gates. And contrary to the age-old local dictum *Mi casa es su casa*, these barriers say, *Mi casa es mi casa*!

A DOWNTOWN TRANSFORMED FOR TOURISTS

It's hard to believe that little more than thirty years ago Santa Fe had a downtown that was a functional city center. Within a three-block radius of the Plaza, children were born at St. Vincent Hospital; baptized at the Cathedral; and attended elementary, middle, and high school. On their way home they might have stopped in the Plaza for a soda at Zook's Pharmacy or a snack at the counter at Woolworth's. Housewives shopped for groceries at Batrite's, Piggly Wiggly, and Safeway, filled their prescriptions at Central and Capital pharmacies, and bought clothes at J. C. Penney, Bell's, and Dunlap's, shoes at Pfluger's and Kahn's, and notions at Taichert's. They looked for fashions at La Tienda and Levine's, and bought appliances at the Maytag shop and furniture at Montoya's and Livingston's. Everyone could mail letters from the old post office opposite the Cathedral, find a plumber at Cartwright's, and get lumber and hardware at Big Jo's. There was a gas station on almost every corner, a tire store on Lincoln Avenue, places to get your shoes repaired, and a choice of three movie theaters on West San Francisco Street. And the Plaza was where locals met old friends and paused to chat. Those days are gone.

Left: **San Francisco Street looking east from the Santa Fe Plaza, 1965. (MNM #43378)**
Top Right: **West San Fransico Street, 1933. (Detail of MNM #51463)** Right: **Santa Fe Plaza, 1912. (MNM #139151)**

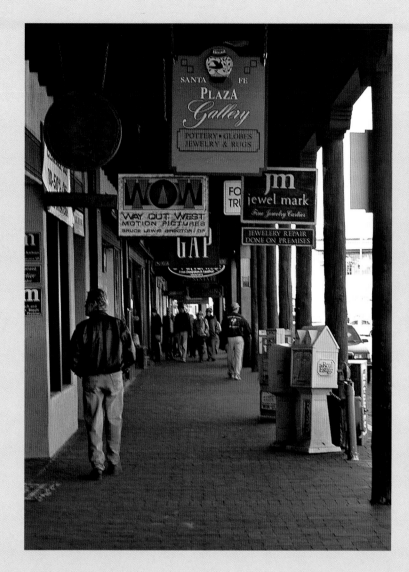

Beginning in the mid-1970s, the downtown began to shift toward upscale tourism. Since then rents have skyrocketed, many small, locally owned shops have been forced out, garages and gas stations have been converted to gift shops and galleries, and the Plaza area has ceased to be the center of community life.

Today average Santa Feans rarely venture downtown. They no longer watch the day pass by from a Plaza bench. Chance meetings take place at Wal-Mart, the supermarket, and the mall. These days the Plaza almost exclusively serves tourists. Hundreds of shops sell paintings, pottery, sculpture, Native American jewelry, and ethnic imports from all corners of the globe, not to mention T-shirts, sweatshirts, and anything else that can be silk-screened with the words "Santa Fe." The only authentic attraction is the presence of Native

Americans who sell their jewelry, pottery, and other art forms under the *portal* of the Palace of the Governors. Scattered about are branches of predictable national chains, and rounding out the Plaza-area economy are expensive hotels and a host of restaurants. All of this comes to a peak at the end of the summer when the city is jammed with thousands of visitors attending the annual Indian Market who leave millions of dollars in their wake.

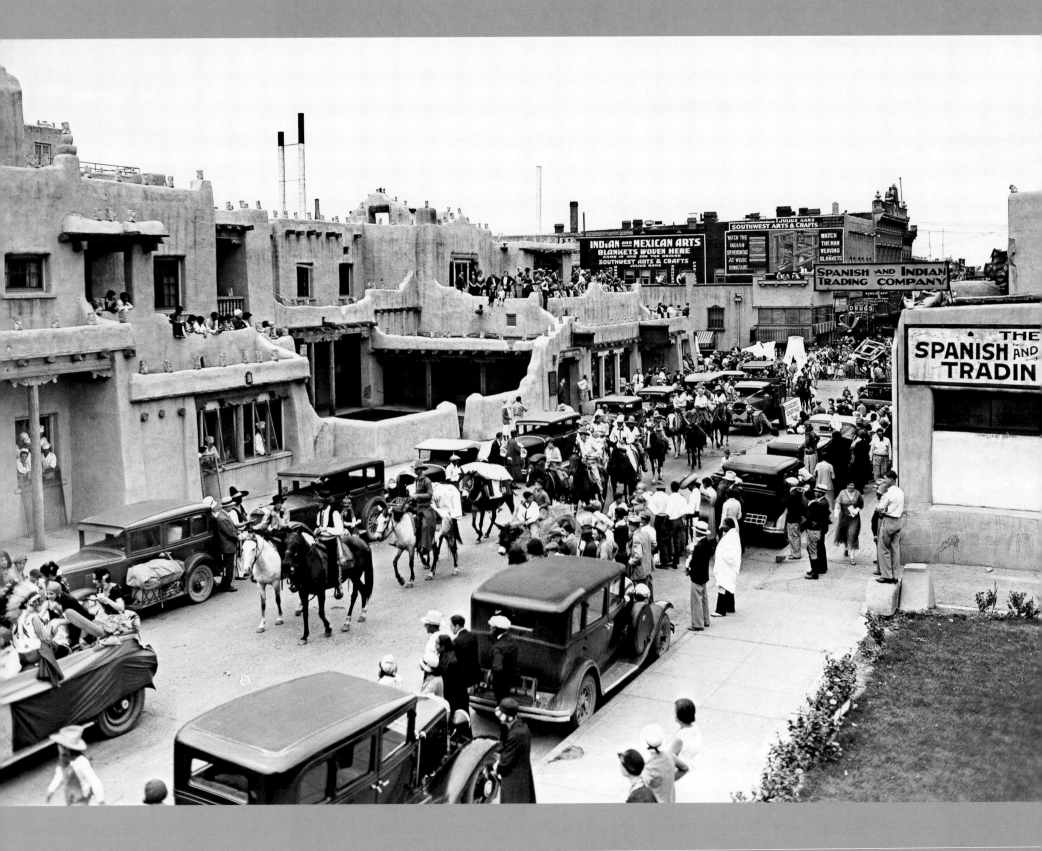

Left: **Fiesta parade, East San Francisco Street. (MNM #118249)**

CHAPTER 8

FOREVER SANTA FE

DESPITE THE VAST RECENT CHANGES AND THE PRESSURES THAT SWARMS OF NEW ARRIVALS HAVE EXERTED ON THEIR COMMUNITY, NATIVE SANTA FEANS CONTINUE TO PRESERVE THEIR TRADITIONAL CULTURE AND WAY OF LIFE, FOCUSED ON FAITH AND FAMILY. THE CHURCH STILL HOLDS THE COMMUNITY TOGETHER, AND TIME IS MARKED BY THE SEASONS AND HOLIDAYS. RELIGIOUS CELEBRATIONS GO ON AS THEY HAVE FOR ALMOST 400 YEARS. SPECIAL EVENTS INCLUDING THE ANNUAL SANTA FE FIESTA, SPANISH MARKET, AND VARIOUS RELIGIOUS PROCESSIONS STILL BRING LOCAL PEOPLE DOWN TO THE PLAZA TO CELEBRATE THEIR HERITAGE AND PASS THE TRADITIONS ON TO THE NEXT GENERATION.

CHAPELS, SHRINES, AND MURALS

Many devout Santa Feans still have altars in their homes, *ofrendas* on a shelf or ledge above the fireplace, a *nicho* carved into a wall holding a statue of a saint, chapels and shrines on their property, and religious murals on their walls. The predominant image is that of Our Lady of Guadalupe, who is rendered in a wide variety of media: painted on the wall of a house, formed by a mosaic of tiles, or cut from tin. Outdoor devotional sites range from full-scale chapels fashioned from stone to a shrine made from an upturned bath tub framing a portrait of Jesus. Carefully crafted and lovingly maintained crosses with flowers called *descansos* (or resting places) mark the sites along streets and roadsides where loved ones have died.

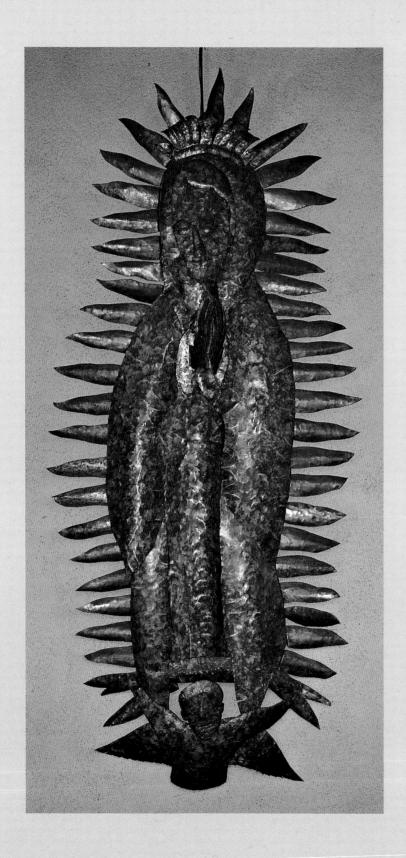

FIESTA DE SANTA FE

In 1712 city authorities decreed that a fiesta be held every September to commemorate the reoccupation of Santa Fe in 1692 by Don Diego de Vargas. Although held sporadically over the next two hundred years, it finally took hold in the 1920s and is today the city's primary celebration. Essentially a three-day affair, it is a combination of religious observances, historic reenactments, theatrical performances, and parades. It features traditional foods, costumes, dance, and music. One of the highlights is the burning of Zozobra. Designed in 1926 by artist Will Shuster, the giant puppet represents Old Man Gloom. His burning before a huge throng of families and revelers symbolizes the shedding of the past year's woes and marks the opening of the Fiesta celebrations. On Saturday morning children gather with their pets for the annual Pet Parade. Presentations using animals, costumes, signs, and other props sometimes take on local themes or express everyday childhood fantasies. On Sunday afternoon the annual Historical/ Hysterical Parade makes its way around the Plaza. Politicos come out in droves to toss candy to their constituents, and elaborate floats celebrate all sorts of organizations, dramatize historical events, and satirize current issues.

Opposite Page: **The burning of Zozobra during the Santa Fe Fiesta. (Detail of MNM #47328)** This Page: **Santa Fe Fiesta Historical/ Hysterical Parade.**

Above and Right: **Music and historic pageantry are an important part of Fiesta activities.**

Opposite Page: **Local people gather on the Plaza dressed in their Fiesta finery.** Above: **Group in front of Museum of Fine Arts during Santa Fe Fiesta. (MNM #117680)**

This Page: **Annual Fiesta Pet Parade.**

This Page: **Floats in the Historical/Hysterical Parade highlight historical events, cultural themes, local issues, and the activities of community organizations.**

RELIGIOUS PROCESSIONS

Below: **Corpus Christi Procession, Palace Avenue, 1895. (MNM #7854)** Right: **Parish priests lead** *La Conquistadora* **Procession down Guadalupe Street.**

Historically, religious processions have been an important part of community life. One of them is Corpus Christi, celebrated in Catholic communities around the world. Others include the Fiesta mass and procession, the candlelight walk to the cross of the martyrs ending Fiesta, and the mass and procession for Spanish Market. Another uniquely Santa Fe procession is that which honors *La Conquistadora*, the small statue representing "the Blessed Mother," which was saved during the Pueblo Revolt of 1680, carried down to El Paso, and returned to Santa Fe after de Vargas reoccupied the city. She is the symbol of Hispanic unity, and many consider her the patron saint of New Mexico. Over the centuries she has been known by different names to reflect the changing spiritual needs and yearnings of the local people. Today she is known as "Our Lady of Peace." Every year she is carried from St. Francis Cathedral to Rosario Chapel (located in Rosario Cemetery, near the site of de Vargas's encampment).

With much pomp and ceremony, music, and recitation of prayers, the procession is led by priests, who are followed by Santa Fe's annual Fiesta royalty and representatives from each of the city's parishes identified by colorful banners. A mass is celebrated in Rosario Chapel that afternoon, and a 6 a.m. mass is offered there on each of the next six days by a pastor from each of the city's parishes. A week later another procession returns *La Conquistadora* to her chapel inside the Cathedral.

Above: **The Fiesta Queen and her court participate in the annual *La Conquistadora* Procession.**
Right: **Members of local churches carry banners representing their parishes.**

Left: **Procession participants carry *La Conquistadora* to and from Rosario Chapel.**
Above: **Musicians and local parishioners accompany *La Conquistadora*.**

Santo. Niño. de Atocha.

SPANISH MARKET

In 1926 the first Spanish Market was held on Santa Fe's Plaza. For almost eighty years this annual event has continued to showcase hundreds of Hispanic artists and craftsmen who work in traditional Spanish colonial art forms. The media and styles on display date to New Mexico's colonial era, and the market serves to perpetuate the unique traditions that grew out of the isolation of that period. Many families representing three or more generations offer for sale everything from carved *santos*, carved and painted *bultos*, painted *retablos*, tin crosses and picture and mirror frames, and straw appliqué crosses to furniture, weavings and other textiles, and objects made of silver and iron. Many of the themes are steeped in the iconography of the Catholic Church, indicating the continued importance of religion in the lives of local people. A special Spanish Market Mass is held at St. Francis Cathedral. Throughout the weekend visitors enjoy traditional food, music, dancing, and costumes.

Various mariachi groups entertain throughout the weekend of Spanish Market.

One of the more popular aspects of Spanish Market is the traditional food.

Both Pages: **Hispanic artists of all ages offer a wide range of traditional art in a variety of media including** *santos*, *bultos*, *retablos*, **weavings, crosses, hammered-tin frames and mirrors, and traditional New Mexican furniture.**

Above: **Patio at Sena Plaza, originally a family hacienda. (MNM #51558)**

CHAPTER 9

OLD WORLD CHARM

Santa Fe maintains a strong connection to its past. The Plaza is still considered the heart of the town, the Cathedral is still the most dignified structure, and the mountains and the light embrace the city as they did 400 years ago. It is a city of mystery and surprises. It is a city of sun and shade, a city of *portales*, a city of the casual encounter. Santa Fe is a city of Old World charm.

Above: *Portal* of the Palace of the Governors, 1924. (MNM #10598)

A CITY OF PORTALES

The Laws of the Indies stipulated that city founders
ring the buildings facing the plaza with *portales* to
provide residents with shelter from sun, snow, and
rain and to offer a congenial place to meet, talk, and
conduct trade. Santa Fe was no exception, and the
Colonial style *portales* remained in place until the
late nineteenth century when many of the early
adobe buildings around the Plaza were replaced by
far grander brick Victorian ones. By that time, in a
bid for New Mexican statehood, the city was trying
to project an all-American image, and for the next
thirty years it did what it could to shed its Pueblo/
Spanish/Mexican heritage and appearance.

But once the city fathers embraced the Spanish/
Pueblo restoration of the downtown after 1912, the
pendulum swung in the opposite direction, the
American influences were stripped off, and the buildings were plastered with brown stucco. By the early
1930s, John Gaw Meem began a lobbying effort to
bring back the *portales,* and by the late 1960s they
once again encircled the Plaza. Today pedestrians are
protected by covered sidewalks throughout the
downtown core and *portales* remain an important
element of residential architecture as well. In many
houses they provide sheltered outdoor living and
working spaces, some of which are well furnished
and even equipped with daybeds and fireplaces.

Above: **Residential *portal* at Casa San Ysidro.**

Left: *Portal* at the Old Post Office/Federal Building. (MNM #112154)

ART IS IN THE AIR

Santa Fe is a city of art, from the religious vernacular expressions of devout Catholics seen all over town to the murals of Chicano history to the unique creative expressions of Native American artists to the special touches of imaginative builders to the public display of work by gallery artists. Santa Fe, long touted as the country's third-largest art market, has galleries on virtually every downtown corner. In addition to the Plaza area, Santa Fe has an entire street, Canyon Road (and its ever-growing number of tributaries), devoted to the sale of every imaginable artistic medium.

BEAUTY AND MYSTERY

Santa Fe is still the most unusual city in the country, more foreign than American, more South American than North American. While government officials conduct meetings in English, they stand prepared to provide for translation into Spanish or Native American languages. The local culture is a rare, unpretentious island in a sea of wanton materialism. Here one is still judged more by his character than his collateral. A gulf exists between most newcomers and native Santa Feans, but it can be bridged. And it is in the people that you'll find the true essence of Santa Fe.

Many old vernacular neighborhoods are in themselves works of art. With winding dirt streets shaded by towering trees and framed by adobe walls, they exude a sense of balance and peace that can draw you back through the centuries.

Plaza Balantine. (Detail of MNM #191921)

The earthiness of the past prevails in the consciousness of today. It echoes through the originality of form, the creative mix of natural materials, the soft, earthy quality of garden walls, and the uniquely handcrafted doors and gates in all the beauty of their imperfection.

CHRISTMAS IN SANTA FE

Center: **The annual Las Posadas celebration.**

Few moments capture the spirit of Santa Fe better than Christmas. With the tang of *piñon* fires hanging in the chilly air, it is a time for family, faith, and favorite foods, a time when the community comes together to celebrate old customs. One of the favorites, which unfolds in Santa Fe's Plaza, is Las Posadas, a pageant with roots that stretch back 400 years to old Mexico. A couple portraying Mary and Joseph move around the darkened Plaza in search of a place to stay, their way lit by a crowd carrying candles. People dressed in colorful

robes and *ponchos* follow and sing carols in Spanish to the accompaniment of a collection of guitars. At each stop along the way, Mary and Joseph are chased away by a devil with the same answer: "No room!" The crowd responds with boos and hisses and the couple moves on to the next stop. Finally they come to the big wooden doors facing Lincoln Avenue that open into the courtyard of the Palace of the Governors. There they are told, "Yes," the large doors swing open, and inside there is hot cider for all.

Above: **The Santa Fe Plaza lit up for Christmas.**

Top: **La Fonda Hotel decorated with** *farolitos*. **(MNM #54312)**
Bottom: **An old pick-up truck decked out in Christmas lights.**

Another favorite custom is to line the walls and walks of Canyon Road, Acequia Madre, and nearby streets with *farolitos* – paper bags of sand lit with candles. At various points, bonfires burn and strollers stop to warm their hands, sip hot drinks, and sing carols.

Christmas in Santa Fe is a time to pause, to rest, to say a blessing, and to give thanks. To be in Santa Fe at Christmas is to feel a kinship with a spirit of humility that has lingered over the city for four centuries.

How to define Santa Fe style has long plagued travel writers, advertising executives, clothing manufacturers, furniture copycats, mass marketers, and even new arrivals sending messages home to describe their surroundings. That's because Santa Fe is an essence, not a style. It is a way of life and a set of values, not a marketable item. In the end, the concept of Santa Fe style is indefinable. It can be captured only in the fragments that define the whole. Santa Fe style is about learning to live the way locals do. And when you have learned how to do that, you begin to live every day as it comes, you learn to value the richness of ordinary life, and that makes a little seem like a lot.

Left: **Santa Fe Plaza in the snow. (MNM #61456)**

Private home on Aqua Fría
Street. (MNM #15252)

ACKNOWLEDGMENTS

We'd like to thank the following people who helped bring this book to fruition:

Thanks to Rina Swentzell, whose sensitivity and knowledge of the Pueblo world and the relationship between it and the surrounding world helped us develop the first chapter as well as the larger context of the book. Also for being a wonderful friend and a constant source of encouragement.

Thanks to Bonita Barlow for her insights, her artistic eye, her unique perspective, her words of wisdom, her wonderful photographs, and her support and friendship.

Thanks to Arthur Olivas and Richard Rudisill and their more than sixty years of combined knowledge of the Museum of New Mexico's Photo Archives. Their help was invaluable.

Thanks to Bill and Athena Steen, who helped us frame the original concept.

Thanks to María Cristina López, Robert Torrez, and Porfirio Sanchez for their insight into the history, culture, customs, and contributions of the Mexican period.

Thanks to the family of Jesús and Teresa Rios, who have taught us the deeper meaning of life in Santa Fe, for allowing us to share their lives and for always making a loving place for us at their table.

Thanks to Gloria Mendoza for sharing her stories, traditions, memories, and friendship.

Thanks to Valentin Valdez, who has always had the time and generosity to share himself and his stories with those like us who want to learn about the rich traditions of Santa Fe and its history.

Thanks to Dolores Martinez for her enthusiasm, support, and encouragement.

Thanks to Beverley Spears for all the work she has done documenting the architectural history of Santa Fe.

Thanks to Robb Lucas for his kindness in allowing us to photograph items from the Trading Post collection at the Wheelwright Museum. Thanks for his permission and his patience.

Speaking of patience, we owe a big thanks to Debbie Uribe at Gibbs Smith, Publisher, who always went out of her way to find the answer to whatever question came up.

This book could never have happened without the unflagging support and consistent faith of Suzanne Taylor, our editor at Gibbs Smith, to whom we give thanks.

We also thank our many photographers for their generous contributions, their time, and their talent.

And a special thanks to Colleen, Adam, and Jared for their patience and understanding in sacrificing their husband and father for the time it took Peter to design and assemble this book.

CONTRIBUTING PHOTOGRAPHERS

BONITA BARLOW is an artist living in Hillsboro, New Mexico. For a decade she has painted this southern New Mexico village from one end to the other in exchange for food. The bigger world awaits her, but she doesn't know how or when she'll answer the call.

BEN CHRISMAN is an independent photographer based in Santa Fe, New Mexico. He has worked at several newspapers in the state and is now focusing his efforts on international news events while also photographing local weddings. His work can be viewed at www.benchrisman.com.

MARTHA COOPER is a documentary photographer who has specialized in shooting urban vernacular art and architecture for more than twenty years. Her photographs have been widely exhibited in museums and galleries and published in magazines and newspapers throughout the world. She is the director of photography at City Lore, the New York Center for Urban Folk Culture.

DICK FRANCIS has been an award-winning professional photographer in Albuquerque, New Mexico, since 1995. Prior to that he worked as a plant ecologist. His photographs have been published in *Collector's Guide*, *Su Casa*, *DESIGNER/builder*, *Rangelands*, *Early New Mexican Furniture*, *Japanese 35mm SLR Cameras*, and *Design Line*. Examples of his work may be viewed at www.fotoswest.com.

LOIS ELLEN FRANK is a New Mexico-based photographer, author, and chef who has spent more than sixteen years documenting the foods and lifeways of the Native Americans of the Southwest. She is the author of *Foods of the Southwest Indian Nations* (Ten Speed Press, 2002), which won the James Beard Award in the Americana category. She has contributed to more than fifteen culinary posters and eighteen cookbooks. And she has taken photographs for some of the best-known restaurateurs and food companies in the country.

STEVE LARESE's photographs have appeared in *National Geographic Traveler*, *National Geographic Adventure*, *The Boston Globe*, *Old House Interiors*, *Arts & Antiques*, *New Mexico Magazine*, and hundreds of other publications. Based in Albuquerque, Larese has earned a reputation for artistic photography in a historical context. More of his work may be seen at www.stevelarese.com.

JONATHAN MICAH REEVES (1984-2005) was born in Santa Fe, where he grew up with his grandparents. He took photography classes at the New Mexico Academy of Sciences and Mathematics and the Santa Fe Photography Workshops.

Parade watchers in front
of El Oñate Theater, 1921.
(Detail of MNM #10661)

PHOTO CREDITS

BONITA BARLOW

Page 13, Page 26 bottom, Page 39, Page 41, Page 45 right, Page 47, Page 59, Page 60, Page 63, Page 69 top left, Page 69 bottom right, Page 72, Page 92, Page 95 top left, Page 109 bottom middle, Page 125 top, Page 155 right, Page 192 middle top, Page 193, Page 213, Page 215, Page 220, Page 222, Page 224, Page 225, Page 226, Page 228 right, Page 229, Page 230

WESLEY BRADFIELD

Page 131, Page 147, Page 164 bottom left

B. BRIXNER

Page 78

NICHOLAS BROWN

Page 42

WILLIAM H. BROWN

Page 112 bottom right

INA SIZER CASSIDY

Page 134

BEN CHRISMAN

Page 232 and 233 center, Page 233 right, Page 236 top, Page 236 bottom

MARTHA COOPER

Page 97 center, Page 188, Page 189, Page 190 right, Page 191 left, Page 191 right

MILDRED T. CREWS

Page 65

EDWARD S. CURTIS

Page 12, Page 20, Page 21, Page 22, Page 29 top, Page 32 left, Page 33 left, Page 37 left

HOPE A. CURTIS

Page 143, Page 144 left, Page 144 and 145 center, Page 145 right

TYLER DINGEE

Page 31, Page 161

ADDISON DOTY

Page 82 right

DICK FRANCIS

Page 68 right, Page 84, Page 85 left, Page 85 top right, Page 86 top, Page 86 bottom left, Page 86 bottom center, Page 86 bottom right, Page 89

LOIS ELLEN FRANK

Page 95 top middle, Page 95 bottom right, Page 96 top left, Page 96 bottom right, Page 97 top left, Page 97 middle left, Page 97 bottom right

BURTON FRASHER

Page 30

JERILOU HAMMETT

Page 32 right, Page 35 top, Page 49 left, Page 108 right, Page 173, Page 174, Page 175, Page 180 top, Page 180 bottom, Page 192 top right, Page 200 right, Page 205 top right, Page 208, Page 209, Page 218 left, Page 223 left, Page 228 right

KINGSLEY HAMMETT

Page 49 top right, Page 51 bottom left, Page 51 bottom right, Page 52 bottom left,

Page 68 left, Page 69 top right, Page 69 bottom left, Page 70 right, Page 73 left, Page 73 right, Page 91, Page 95 middle right, Page 107 middle top, Page 107 top right, Page 107 bottom right, Page 108 top left, Page 108 top middle left, Page 108 bottom middle left, Page 108 bottom left, Page 109 bottom left, Page 124 left, Page 125 bottom left, Page 125 bottom right, Page 154 left, Page 154 top right, Page 154 middle, Page 154 bottom right, Page 160, Page 165, Page 176 and 177 top, Page 176 bottom left, Page 177 bottom right, Page 179 top, Page 179 bottom, Page 181, Page 184 all, Page 185 left, Page 185 right, Page 187, Page 190 left, Page 192 left (Ray Herrera tinwork), Page 192 middle bottom, Page 192 bottom right, Page 195, Page 197 top left, page 197 bottom left, Page 197 bottom middle, Page 197 bottom right, Page 198 all, Page 203, Page 204 all, Page 205 left, Page 205 bottom right, Page 206 left, Page 206 right, Page 207, Page 210, Page 211 top left, Page 211 bottom left, Page 219, Page 221, Page 231 left, Page 231 right, Page 234, Page 235 bottom

Following Page: *Music In the Plaza* by John Sloan. (Detail of MNM #40881)